INVENTING THE FLAT EARTH

Other Books by Jeffrey Burton Russell

Dissent and Reform in the Early Middle Ages (1965)

Medieval Civilization (1968)

A History of Medieval Christianity: Prophecy and Order (1968)

Religious Dissent in the Middle Ages (1970)

Witchcraft in the Middle Ages (1972)

The Devil: Perceptions of Evil from Antiquity to Primitive Christianity (1977)

A History of Witchcraft: Sorcerers, Heretics, Pagans (1980)

Medieval Heresies: A Bibliography (with Carl Berkhout) (1981)

Satan: The Early Christian Tradition (1981)

Lucifer: The Devil in the Middle Ages (1984)

Mephistopheles: The Devil in the Modern World (1986)

The Prince of Darkness: Radical Evil and the Power of Good in History (1988)

Ruga in aevis (with Madeleine L'Engle and Kathleen Drake) (1990)

INVENTING THE FLAT EARTH

COLUMBUS AND MODERN HISTORIANS

Jeffrey Burton Russell

Foreword by David Noble

PRAEGER

New York
Westport, Connecticut
London

Library of Congress Cataloging-in-Publication Data

Russell, Jeffrey Burton.
    Inventing the flat earth : Columbus and modern historians /
  Jeffrey Burton Russell : foreword by David Noble.
      p. cm.
    Includes bibliographical references and index.
    ISBN 0-275-93956-1 (alk. paper)
    1. Columbus, Christopher—Influence. 2. Cosmography. 3. America—
Discovery and exploration—Spanish. I. Title.
E112.R93   1991   91-67

British Library Cataloguing in Publication Data is available.

Library of Congress Catalog Card Number: 91-67
ISBN: 0-275-93956-1

First published in 1991

Praeger Publishers, One Madison Avenue, New York, NY 10010
An imprint of Greenwood Publishing Group, Inc.

Printed in the United States of America

The paper used in this book complies with the
Permanent Paper Standard issued by the National
Information Standards Organization (Z39.48-1984).

10 9 8 7 6 5 4 3 2 1

Sarah and Xoco: Sorori filiaeque

Contents

Illustrations follow page 50.

Foreword

Jeffrey Burton Russell, who has published extensively on the intellectual history of the medieval world, has now turned his attention to the intellectual history of the modern world. In *Inventing the Flat Earth* he presents modern readers with a marvelously stimulating analysis of the powerful conventions that are used to define the difference between the medieval and the modern. The great irony present in his analysis is that it subverts that conventional understanding.

At the beginning of his book he quotes from current textbooks used in American grade schools, high schools, and colleges which insist that there was a consensus among medieval scholars from A.D. 300 to 1492 that the earth was flat. This also was the thesis of the influential historian Daniel Boorstin writing for a popular audience in his book, *The Discoverers*, published in 1983. Russell then uses his deep knowledge of medieval intellectual history to demonstrate that the opposite was true. It was conventional wisdom among both early- and late-medieval thinkers that the world was round.

According to what Russell calls the modern Flat Earth Error, it was the courage of the rationalist Christopher Columbus that began the liberation of modern people from the superstitions of the Catholic church. His voyage in 1492 supposedly destroyed the irrational mythology of the Dark Ages by empirically dem-

onstrating that the world was round, not flat. Although it was
Europeans participating in the Renaissance and Reformation
who invented the idea that there was a thousand years of darkness between the classical world and a new modern world, Russell believes that the Flat Earth Error did not become a modern
orthodoxy until the nineteenth century. He finds its beginning
in the writings of the American Washington Irving and the
Frenchman Antoine-Jean Letronne. But it became widespread
conventional wisdom from 1870 to 1920 as a result of "the war
between science and religion," when for many intellectuals in
Europe and the United States all religion became synonymous
with superstition and science became the only legitimate source
of truth. It was during the last years of the nineteenth century
and the early years of the twentieth century, then, that the voyage of Columbus became such a widespread symbol of the futil-
ity of the religious imagination and the liberating power of
scientific empiricism.

The further irony for Russell is that as soon as the modern
myth of Columbus as the pioneer who proved the error of medieval mythology became orthodoxy, the historians who were
studying the medieval world during the 1920s began to present
empirical evidence for the falsity of the modern Flat Earth
myth. Soon the emerging field of the history of science pro-
vided further evidence that medieval thinkers, like the classical
thinkers before them, believed the earth was round. But as
Russell points out, the evidence presented by medieval historians and historians of science for the last seventy years has not
undermined the persuasive power of the modern myth that medieval thinkers believed the earth was flat. The explanation of
this pattern for Russell is that the Flat Earth Error is part of a
much larger modern faith in progress. "Our determination to
believe the Flat Error," he writes, "arises out of contempt for the
past and our need to believe in the superiority of the present."

Russell's book should be read in conjunction with another
new book, Anthony Kemp's *The Estrangement from the Past*
(1991). Kemp is concerned with how modern people have

found meaning in time once they rejected the medieval sense of unity. He shares Russell's belief that when time is conceived in discontinuous terms, it becomes necessary to believe in progress to escape the terror of a world without meaning. As Russell so eloquently has written, "The terror of meaninglessness, of falling off the edge of knowledge is greater than the imagined fear of falling off the edge of the earth. And so we prefer to believe a familiar error than to search, unceasingly, the darkness." This, then, is the great challenge of Russell's book. He asks that we modern readers stop considering our world as superior to other human communities that have existed or will exist. Only a historian who is in command of the intellectual histories of both the medieval and modern worlds could write such a provocative and persuasive book.

David Noble

Preface

The almost universal supposition that educated medieval people believed the earth to be flat puzzled me and struck me as dissonant when I was in elementary school, but I assumed that teacher knew best and shelved my doubts. By the time my children were in elementary school, they were learning the same mistake, and by that time I knew it was a falsehood. Most of the undergraduates I have taught at the University of California have received the same misinformation — from schoolbooks, storybooks, cinema, and television. The Flat Error is firmly fixed in our minds; I hope this book will do a little to help dislodge it. "The round earths imagin'd corners" (Donne) always were imaginary.

I want to thank the following people who have helped enormously with this book in one way or another: Joseph Amato, Lawrence Badash, Morton Gibian, Anita Guerrini, Christine Gulish, Paul Hernadi, Lois Huneycutt, Lauren Helm Jared, Walter Kaufmann, David Lindberg, Leonard Marsak, David Noble, Michael Osborne, Janet Pope, Norman Ravitch, Diana Russell, Jan Ryder, A. Mark Smith, John Talbott, Waldo Tobler, Jack Vizzard, and Robert Westmann. Christine Gulish is the best research assistant I have ever known. Jan Ryder was generous with her time and comments. My dear friends Morton Gibian and Walter Kaufmann helped, the first by be-

ing stubbornly curious and the second by performing an imper-
sonation of a Yiddish Columbus that is tempting to recount but
might provoke yet another Error. I am most grateful to David
Noble for his kind interest and willingness to write the foreword. My greatest thanks go to Joe Amato, without whose en-
couragement this book might well have never appeared.

CHAPTER ONE

The Well-Rounded Planet

Eight o'clock in the morning, August 3, 1992, marks a full half-millennium since Christopher Columbus set off on his first voyage to the New World, an occasion honored in the United States by the Congressional Quincentenary Jubilee Act of 1987. In the United States, the tone of the observance of 1992 contrasts with the joyous imperial celebration of 1892, because the dark side of Columbus's voyage comes to mind in a way that it did not a century ago. Native Americans may regard 1492 as the beginning of their disinheritance and African-Americans as the opening of the largest market for black slaves. Jews and Muslims may remember that 1492 was also the year of their expulsion from Spain by Ferdinand and Isabella, the very monarchs who sponsored Columbus. Hispanic-Americans may recall the colonial period with more grief than nostalgia. Beyond the immediate and pressing need to re-evaluate the impact of the opening of the Americas to Europe is another, curious problem, in its way as ethnocentric as the imperialism of 1892.

Five hundred years after Columbus (1451–1506), his story continues to be accompanied by a curious and persistent illusion: the well-known fable that Columbus discovered America and proved that the earth is round, to the astonishment of his contemporaries, who believed that it was flat and that one might sail off the edge. It is an illusion by no means confined to the uneducated. John Huchra, of the Harvard-Smithsonian Institute for Astrophysics, was quoted as saying:

> Back then [when the New World was discovered] there was a lot of theoretical, yet incorrect, knowledge about what the world was like. Some thought the world might be flat and you could fall off the edge, but the explorers went out and found what was truly there.[1]

To put it in other words: it is falsely supposed that one purpose, and certainly one result, of Columbus's voyage was to prove to medieval, European skeptics that the earth was round. In reality there were no skeptics. All educated people throughout Europe knew the earth's spherical shape and its approximate circumference. This fact has been well established by historians for more than half a century.

One of the most eminent contemporary historians of science, David Lindberg, said:

> In the usual story, theoretical dogma regarding a flat earth had to be overcome by empirical evidence for its sphericity. The truth is that the sphericity of the earth was a central feature of theoretical dogma as it came down to the Middle Ages — so central that no amount of contrary theoretical or empirical argumentation could conceivably have dislodged it.[2]

In 1964 C. S. Lewis had written, "Physically considered, the earth is a globe; all the authors of the high Middle Ages are agreed on this. . . . The implications of a spherical earth were fully grasped."[3] And Cecil Jane had already declared in the 1930s:

> By the middle of the fifteenth century, the sphericity of the globe was accepted as a fact by all, or at the very least by almost all,

educated men throughout western Europe. There is no foundation for the assertion, which was once credited, that in Spain a
contrary view was maintained by orthodox theologians and supported by religious prejudice.[4]

The question then is where the illusion — "The Flat Error" —
came from and why educated people continue to believe it. The
Error is not the alleged medieval belief that the earth was flat,
but rather the modern error that such a belief ever prevailed.[5]
This Flat Error remains popular. It is still found in many
textbooks and encyclopedias.[6] A 1983 textbook for fifth-graders
reports, "[Columbus] felt he would eventually reach the Indies
in the East. Many Europeans still believed that the world was
flat. Columbus, they thought, would fall off the earth."[7]
A 1982 text for eighth-graders said:

> The European sailor of a thousand years ago also had many
> other strange beliefs [besides witches and the Devil]. He turned
> to these beliefs because he had no other way to explain the dan-
> gers of the unknown sea. He believed . . . that a ship could sail
> out to sea just so far before it fell off the edge of the sea. . . . The
> people of Europe a thousand years ago knew little about the
> world.[8]

A prestigious text for college students informs them that the
fact that the earth is round was known to the ancient Greeks
but lost in the Middle Ages.[9] Literature follows suit. Joseph
Chiari's play, *Christopher Columbus,* contains this dialogue between Columbus and a Prior:

> Columbus: The Earth is not flat, Father, it's round!
> The Prior: Don't say that!
> Columbus: It's the truth; it's not a mill pond strewn with islands,
> it's a sphere.
> The Prior: Don't, don't say that; it's blasphemy.[10]

By the 1980s, a large number of textbooks and encyclopedias had corrected the story,[11] but the Flat Error was restated in a widely read book by the former Librarian of Congress, Daniel Boorstin, *The Discoverers* (1983). Boorstin wrote:

> A Europe-wide phenomenon of scholarly amnesia . . . afflicted the continent from A.D. 300 to at least 1300. During those centuries Christian faith and dogma suppressed the useful image of the world that had been so slowly, so painfully, and so scrupulously drawn by ancient geographers.[12]

He called this alleged hiatus the "Great Interruption." His fourteenth chapter, "A Flat Earth Returns," derided the "legion of Christian geographers" who followed the geographical path marked out by a sixth-century eccentric.[13] In fact the eccentric Cosmas Indicopleustes had no followers whatever: his works were ignored or dismissed with derision throughout the Middle Ages.[14]

How could Boorstin disseminate the Flat Error and the public accept it uncritically? The detective work on that question produces a result more frightening than the idea of falling off the edge of the earth: it is the idea of falling off the edge of knowledge.

The very statement that "Columbus proved the world was round" presents logical difficulties. Since Columbus did not ever sail around the world, it was not until Magellan's men came back from circumnavigating the globe in 1522 that the sphericity of the planet could be absolutely proved *empirically.* So, if Columbus's feat can be said to have been any kind of proof at all, it must be in the sense that it convinced people that the earth was *probably* round, people who until then had believed otherwise. But no one had believed otherwise.[15]

What is meant by "no one"? No doubt some people alive on August 3, 1492, believed that the earth was flat. Some do today, and not only members of the International Flat Earth Society.

Surveys demonstrate the geographical ignorance of people in the late twentieth century.[16] But the ideas of the uneducated had no effect upon Columbus, or upon his patron Queen Isabella. Why should they have? The educated — geographers and theologians alike — were there to tell them that the earth is round.[17] Those who opposed Columbus's voyage did so on other grounds entirely.

The idea of geocentricity is often linked in the modern mind with the idea of flatness, but the two are separate. With a few exceptions, educated people before Copernicus (1473–1543) in fact believed that the planets — and the stars — revolved around the earth rather than around the sun. However, the idea that the earth is spherical is sharply distinct from the idea that the earth is at the center of the cosmos. A flat earth in no way follows logically from a spherical, geocentric cosmos. But there is one historical way in which the two are connected: by Copernicus in the sixteenth century, who linked them in order to discredit his geocentric opponents.

By the time Copernicus had revolutionized the way people viewed the planets — as revolving around the sun rather than the earth — the seed of the Flat Error had been planted, but it did not grow to choke the truth until much later. When did it triumph and why? Who was responsible? These are the main questions of this book. But the first question is what Columbus and his opponents and contemporaries really thought as opposed to what the Flat Error supposes that they did.

The story of Christopher Columbus, the bold young rationalist who overcame ignorant and intractable churchmen and superstitious sailors, is fixed in modern folklore.

"But, if the world is round," said Columbus, "it is not hell that lies beyond that stormy sea. Over there *must* lie the eastern strand of Asia, the Cathay of Marco Polo, the land of the Kubla Khan, and Cipango, the great island beyond it." "Nonsense!" said the neighbors; "the world isn't round—can't you *see* it is flat? And Cosmas Indicopleustes who lived hundreds of years before you were born, says it is flat; and he got it from the Bible. . . ."

[Columbus at last gains a hearing from the clergy.] In the hall of the convent there was assembled the imposing company— shaved monks in gowns of black and gray, fashionably dressed men from the court in jaunty hats, cardinals in scarlet robes—all the dignity and learning of Spain, gathered and waiting for the man and his idea. He stands before them with his charts, and explains his belief that the world is round. . . . They had heard something of this before at Cordova, and here at Salamanca, be-fore the commission was formally assembled, and they had their arguments ready.

"You think the earth is round, and inhabited on the other side? Are you not aware that the holy fathers of the church have con-demned this belief? . . . Will you contradict the fathers? The Holy Scriptures, too, tell us expressly that the heavens are spread out like a tent, and how can that be true if the earth is not flat like the ground the tent stands on? This theory of yours looks heretical."

Columbus might well quake in his boots at the mention of her-esy; for there was that new Inquisition just in fine running order, with its elaborate bone-breaking, flesh-pinching, thumb-screwing, hanging, burning, mangling system for heretics. What would become of the Idea if he should get passed over to that energetic institution?[18]

The courage of the rationalist confronted by the crushing weight of tradition and its cruel institutions of repression is ap-pealing, exciting—and baseless.[19] Christopher Columbus was less a rationalist than a combination of religious enthusiast and commercial entrepreneur, and he enjoyed the kind of good luck that comes once in a half-millennium. Columbus lived at the right time: the Turks were blocking the old land routes to India and China; the Portuguese were seeking an eastward sea route around Africa and in the process establishing profitable trading posts; the "Catholic Monarchs" Ferdinand and Isabella were uniting Spain and could be persuaded to steal a march on their Portuguese competitors. Columbus argued that a direct route to the East would open China's riches to Catholic merchants and its souls to Catholic missionaries. He was not the last to entertain the illusion that Asians were ready to throw themselves body and soul at the feet of Europeans.

Columbus's speculations about sailing west to the Indies (a term that then meant the entire Far East) was part of a broad front of opinions already advancing in that direction. Columbus read widely and knew that others had argued that between Spain and the Indies the sea was short and could be crossed in a few days.[20] Paolo dal Pozzo Toscanelli, the Florentine astronomer, replied to a letter of 1474 from a canon of Lisbon that a westward voyage was feasible, using islands as watering and provisioning places along the way. He sent him a map showing many small islands in the western sea between Europe and the Indies. Columbus, hearing of the correspondence, obtained a copy of letter and map from Toscanelli. In 1492, the same year that Columbus sailed westward, Martin Behaim, who had visited Lisbon in 1484, returned to his native city of Nuremberg and constructed a globe of the earth showing an open sea westward to Japan and China. In 1493, Hieronymus Munzer wrote to King John II of Portugal to propose the westward journey, unaware that on October 12, 1492, Columbus and his crew had already sighted the island of "San Salvador" (possibly Watling Island in the Bahamas). Columbus believed he was in an archipelago that included Japan.

None of the early sources, including Christopher Columbus's own *Journal* as presented by Las Casas, and Ferdinand Columbus's resume in his *History of the Admiral* of the reasons why his father made the voyage, raises any question about roundness.[21] Neither do the accounts of the Cabots or other explorers before Magellan's circumnavigation. The reason was that there was no question. Whence, then, the lurid accounts of the explorer at bay before his benighted enemies?

In fact Columbus did have opponents. Around 1484, Columbus proposed the voyage to King John of Portugal, but the king preferred to continue south and east along the African coast, a policy that was yielding rich economic rewards, rather than take a chance on the westward passage. When Columbus turned to the Spanish monarchs Ferdinand and Isabella, he found them preoccupied with completing the unification of Spain by conquering the Moorish kingdom of Granada. It is true that the Catholic Monarchs had established the Spanish Inquisition as a State Council in 1483, but that institution, aimed primarily against converted Jews who relapsed into their own religion, had no interest whatever in the shape of the globe.

In addition to the political hesitations, there were intellectual objections. The Spanish monarchs referred Columbus to a royal commission headed by Hernando de Talavera, Queen Isabella's confessor and later Archbishop of Granada.[22] This commission was in effect a secular ad hoc committee composed of both lay and clerical advisers; it was in no sense an ecclesiastical council, let alone an inquisitorial convention. These were practical men trying to establish whether a westward passage was practical.

After delays, Talavera called a rather informal committee meeting at Cordoba in early summer 1486, another at Christmas in Salamanca, and yet another in 1490 in Seville. The commission's meeting at Salamanca was no convention of scholars, and the university was involved only in the sense that the committee met in one of its colleges. Of the objections posed to Columbus, none involved questioning sphericity. Even the strange objection that a person having sailed "down" the curve of the earth might find it difficult to sail "up" it in return assumed sphericity.[23] More convincingly, the opponents, citing the traditional measurements of the globe according to Ptolemy, argued that the circumference of the earth was too great and the distance too far to allow a successful western passage. They rightly feared that life and treasure might be squandered on an impossibly long voyage. The committee adjourned without agreeing, and the Spanish rulers, occupied in their wars against the Moors, gave no reply.

Meanwhile, between 1486 and 1490, Columbus carefully prepared the calculations with which to defend his plans. In 1490 the commission finally decided against him. Again, none of their objections called into question the roundness of the earth. Relying on Ptolemy and Augustine, they argued that the sea was too wide; the curvature of the planet would prohibit return from the other side of the world; there could not be inhabitants on the other side because they would not be descended from Adam; only three of the traditional five climatic zones were habitable; God would not have allowed Christians to remain ignorant of unknown lands for so long.[24]

The committee's doubts were understandable, for Columbus had cooked his own arguments. The modern figure for the circumference of the planet is about 40,000 kilometers (km). The earth is divided latitudinally and longitudinally into 360 degrees, and the length of a degree of latitude could be roughly measured by sightings on the sun, as Eratosthenes had done nearly two millennia earlier; the modern figure is about 111 km. It follows that 1 degree of longitude at the equator is approximately the same figure as 1 degree of latitude.[25] Columbus needed to persuade Ferdinand and Isabella that the journey across the ocean sea was not impossibly long, and to do that he needed to reduce two things: the number of degrees occupied by empty sea, and the distance between degrees.

The standard calculations accepted by most geographers in the fifteenth century were those of Claudius Ptolemy (c. A.D. 150). Ptolemy believed that the planet was covered by the ocean, except for the large, inhabited landmass that he called the *oikoumene* and that we refer to as Eurasia and Africa. Oikoumene will be translated here as "the known world." East to West Ptolemy's known world occupied about 180 degrees, leaving 180 for open sea.[26] But Columbus also read Pierre D'Ailly, who gave a figure of 225 degrees for the land and 135 for the sea.[27] This was much better for Columbus but not yet good enough. Arguing that Marco Polo's travels had shown that the Asian landmass extended eastward much further than was known by Ptolemy or D'Ailly, Columbus added another 28 degrees to the land, making it 253 degrees against 107 for the sea. Since Japan was (Columbus believed from Marco Polo) far to the east of China, he subtracted another 30 degrees from the sea, making it 77. Then, since he planned to leave from the Canary Islands rather than from Spain itself, he subtracted another 9, leaving 68. Even this was not quite enough, and in a final superb gesture, he decided that D'Ailly had been 8 degrees off to begin with. By the time he had done, he had reduced the ocean to 60 degrees, less than one-third the modern figure of 200 degrees for the distance from the Canary Islands westward to Japan.[28]

Not content with bending longitude, Columbus molded the mile. A degree of longitude at the equator is approximately equal to a degree of latitude, and D'Ailly cited the Arabic astronomer Al-Farghani or "Alfragano" (ninth century) as setting a degree of latitude at 56-2/3 miles.[29] This figure was used by Columbus — with a twist. He chose to assume that Alfragano's were the short Roman miles rather than the longer nautical miles. Columbus translated Alfragano's figure into 45 nautical miles. Since Columbus planned to cross the ocean considerably north of the equator, he adjusted this to about 40 nautical miles (about 74 km) per degree.

Putting these figures together, Columbus calculated the distance between the Canaries and Japan at about 4,450 km. The modern figure is 22,000 km. Put another way, he estimated the voyage at about 20 percent its actual length. If God or good luck had not put America — the West Indies — in the way to catch him, Columbus and his crews might indeed have perished, not from falling off the earth but from starvation and thirst. Columbus clinched his argument to his patrons by adding that the voyage could probably be broken at intervening islands.

After long political maneuvering and many disappoint-

ments, Columbus at last in April 1492 obtained Queen Isabella's support and set sail on the third day of August.[30]
Columbus's opponents, misinformed as they were, had more
science and reason on their side than he did on his. He had
political ability, stubborn determination, and courage. They
had a hazy, but fairly accurate, idea of the size of the globe.
How did these allegedly benighted clerics of the Middle Ages
come by such accurate knowledge?

CHAPTER TWO

The Medieval Ball

Fifteenth-century astronomers, geographers, philosophers, and theologians, far from disputing sphericity, wrote sophisticated treatises based on Aristotle and the "Geography" of Ptolemy of Alexandria.[31] Aristotle had argued for a spherical earth surrounded by concentric "crystalline" spheres of planets and stars. The astronomers reviving Ptolemy's cosmology in the fifteenth century created a more complex system of spheres modified by smaller spheres called epicycles and deferents. In geography, Ptolemy was descriptive where Aristotle was abstract; he produced a detailed map of the known world. Some fifteenth-century writers combined Aristotle and Ptolemy with Crates of Mallos (c. 165 B.C.) to produce a system that by the last quarter of the century was accepted in educated circles throughout Europe, including Spain.

The system, in its broad outlines, looked like this. The spherical earth was the center of the cosmos, which was arranged in concentric "spheres" around it. Since the planets and stars were not self-moved bodies, they were assumed to be attached to, or embedded in, the spheres, which carried them around. The closest sphere was that of the moon. Beyond the moon was Mercury, then Venus, then the sun, then Jupiter, then Saturn, and then the fixed stars. In order to account for the peculiar motions of the planets, including retrograde motion, the spheres of the planets were seen not as simple circles but as complexities involving circular deferents centering on the spheres and circular epicycles centered on the deferents. Beyond the sphere of the fixed stars was a *primum mobile,* the outermost moving material sphere, which in turn imparted motion to the whole system of stars and planets.

Returning to the surface of the earth: the earth was roughly divided into quarters. In one quarter was the known world; beyond that was the sea. Opinion was divided as to whether lands in the antipodes (the opposite quarter of the earth) existed. (Some writers took the antipodes to be in the southern hemisphere, others on the opposite side of the northern.) In this respect the existence of another, unknown continent was not unexpected by everyone, although most assumed that the ocean sea probably stretched westward from Iberia all the way to the Indies. Since the world was a huge globe of which the known world represented only about a quarter, that quarter could be projected as a map onto a flat surface; mapmakers were (and still are) experimenting with a variety of possible projections.

Columbus most carefully consulted Pierre D'Ailly (1350–1420), a theologian and philosopher, who discussed the earth's volume, the poles, climatic zones, and the length of degrees.[32] D'Ailly questioned the roundness of the earth only in the modern sense that because of surface irregularities such as mountains and valleys it is only approximately a sphere. Without obstacles, he said, a person could walk around the globe in a few years.

W. G. H. Randles in a brilliant, original study of conceptions of the globe in the late medieval and early modern period, cited Zacharia Lilio as an anomaly. Although Lilio's argument is naive, he does not deny the sphericity of the globe but that of the known world (he confuses *terra* as globe with *terra* as oikoumene and further muddles the argument with the question of antipodeans). Edward Grant's rule that there were no educated people who denied the roundness of the earth in the fifteenth century is correct.[33]

Some modern writers have conceded that the sphericity of the earth was known between the translation of Ptolemy in 1410 and Columbus's voyage, but insist that it was ignored previously. They see the fifteenth century as the age of Humanism and the "Renaissance of learning." Using their guidelines, the alleged edge of darkness, when the true shape of the earth was discovered, recedes from 1492 to 1410.

But what was the educated view before 1410? Around 1250 natural science made enormous progress, a development that encouraged, and was encouraged by, the translation of a number of Greek and Arabic works into Latin in the twelfth century. Every medieval student learned geography as a part of astronomy and geometry, two of the standard "seven liberal arts," and the ideas conveyed by the new translations percolated down into the schools. Roger Bacon (c. 1220–1292) affirmed the roundness of the earth using classical traditional arguments: the sphere is the most perfect shape; the heavens are spherical; the curvature of the earth explains why we can see farther from a higher elevation. The sea is not uncrossable, said Bacon, and inhabitable lands may exist opposite our own.[34]

The greatest scientists of the later Middle Ages, Jean Buridan (c. 1300–1358) and Nicole Oresme (c. 1320–1382), even discussed the rotation of the earthly sphere. Giles of Rome (1247–1316) postulated a globe of water, with the dry land as an irregularity rising above the sea on one side. In this way the world could be *both* flat (the oikoumene, or known world) *and* round (the whole globe).[35]

The so-called "John of Mandeville," a pseudonymous writer in Liège, claimed in his book of *Travels* (c. 1370) to have taken marvelous journeys throughout the world. He was lying, but his lies took place on a round earth: this is why, he says, one can see stars in Sumatra that one cannot see in Europe. When it is day in the antipodes it is midnight in our country, for the Lord made the earth all round in the midst of the firmament. He laughs at "simple people" who think that antipodeans would fall off the other side of the globe.[36]

Insights into the geographical beliefs of the uneducated are usually indirect, but popular literature gives the impression of a general muddle. A few texts are clear, such as the French *Image du monde* (1246–1248), which says that "the world is round like a playing ball; the sky surrounds the earth on all sides like an eggshell." William Caxton translated this work as *The Mirrour of the World* in 1480: Caxton wrote that barring obstacles, a person could walk all around the earth "lyke as a flye goth round aboute a round apple."[37] Brunetto Latini, Dante's teacher, developed the egg image in his *Book of the Treasure* (1266): the earth is at the center like the yolk and is surrounded first by fire, then by air, and then by water; the shell is the quintessence, the "fifth element." Shifting alimentary metaphors, he also remarked that the earth is "round like an apple." The anonymous and popular *Book of Sidrach* asserted that God had made the world in a perfect sphere to mirror his own perfection.[38]

Other texts are ambiguous. Although there is no clear statement of flatness in French medieval literature, there is plenty of confusion. In French as well as in English and Latin the terms "earth," "world," and "round" are imprecise. Béroul's *Tristan,* for example, uses "round" ambiguously for both "round table" and "round earth."[39]

Educated people, and perhaps others, may have "known" that the world was a sphere. Even so, to judge by the passages discussed above, they found the implications of the fact confusing. But there is evidence to suggest that, before 1300 at least, some people in France actually thought of the world as a disc.[40]

This removes the edge of darkness back to 1300 and back among the poorly educated. Most people, then as now, cared more about getting from Laon to Rouen, or from York to Lincoln, than from Portugal to Persia.

Spiritual truth was another concern that outweighed physics in the thirteenth century. Dante (1265–1321), the most philosophical of medieval poets, was so well aware of Ptolemaic astronomy that his *Convivio* offers an estimate of the earth's diameter at 6500 miles. But what he presents in his masterpiece

The Divine Comedy is a cosmos whose physical shape is a metaphor for its spiritual shape. Using a mixture of Ptolemy and Aristotle common in his time, Dante places the spherical earth at the center of the cosmos, surrounded by concentric spheres out to the sphere of the fixed stars. The earth is a perfect sphere — other than the imperfection of its surface caused by the plunging fall of Satan, which hollowed out hell in the center and cast up the mount of purgatory on the other side.

What Dante meant by this is a key to understanding the thirteenth-century worldview. Dante's scheme of the cosmos is meant to be poetic, not scientific. It is not a scientific description, but a *moral description*. The cosmos is arranged in a set of concentric spheres with Satan frozen in immobile darkness at the dead center where all the heavy weight of the cosmos converges, where there can be no motion, no light, no love, no hope. As we rise from hell, we gradually open out to love, light, and joy, until eventually we ascend through the mystic rose to the infinite bright joy of heaven. This is the way the cosmos "really" is, Dante maintains. Dante did not mean this "really" in the sense of physics, geography, or astronomy; he made the physical shape of the cosmos a metaphor of what was more important, more real: its moral and spiritual shape.[41]

Medieval maps did not attempt to conform to criteria set for a modern atlas. "Maps need not necessarily show only Euclidean space."[42] A map is the representation of any concept whatever in spatial terms; there are "maps of the heavens," "maps of the unconscious," "maps of personal finances," "maps of the economy," or "maps of the future."

About 1,100 maps of the earth from the eighth through the fifteenth century survive; they are almost all flat — as are the maps in a modern atlas. Medieval world maps — *mappaemundi* — come in several varieties.[43] Most are circular; many are oval or rectangular. The common circular world maps called "T in O" (T-O) show the T-shaped oikoumene surrounded by the O-shaped sea. One could interpret these maps as a flat wheel or disc, but most were intended to represent only a portion of the sphere—the known world—on a flat map, just as a modern flat map of Europe or Africa is intended to represent only part of the planet.[44] Other medieval maps showed five climatic zones.[45] The purpose of the medieval mappaemundi was not to take a Euclidian snapshot of the size and shape of the earth or its regions, but rather to convey moral truth or sacred or political history. That Jerusalem is set at the center of many T-O maps is not a statement that Jerusalem is at the geometric center of even the known world, much less of the whole earth. Rather, it shows that Jerusalem is the moral and spiritual—the *real*—center of the world.[46] Likewise, a fourteenth-century map showing cities in Christian hands that in fact had fallen to the Turks does not indicate the carelessness or ignorance of the mapmaker, but rather a statement that these cities are *really* Christian in a moral and spiritual sense, more important to the mapmaker than the military or political (or even cultural) sense. Areas that are more important to the mapmaker are often drawn larger than those considered less important. A medieval artist might paint a king much larger than his servant, not because the artist is ignorant of physiology, but because he wishes to show that the king is "really" the greater in the more important, hierarchical sense.[47]

Some modern writers have dismissed the mappaemundi as impractical. How could one sail from Le Havre to Amsterdam using one of these, they ask? No one would have dreamed of trying. The mappaemundi were not meant to be practical. Practical maps from the Middle Ages do exist, and are of two major types; one is the crude but effective sketch that shows, for example, what towns one encounters on a journey between York and London and in what order. The other, widely used from the late thirteenth century, is the navigational "portolan chart," both accurate and detailed, which used longitude and latitude as coordinates. Toward the end of the Middle Ages, the information on the Portolan charts was coordinated with cosmology to produce geographically accurate maps.

So evidence from the maps pushes the "edge of darkness"

back to before 1250. What of the period of scholastic realism
from 1050 to 1275? In the "Treatise on the Sphere" (c. 1250)
Sacrobosco followed the Arab al-Farghani in demonstrating the
roundness of the earth from the observation that the mast of a
departing ship disappears from sight after the hull, that the
stars rise in the east earlier than farther west, and that different
stars are seen in different latitudes.[48] Sacrobosco and his
contemporaries drew upon twelfth-century translations of the
Arabic astronomers and geographers.[49] The scholastic philosophers, including the greatest of them, Thomas Aquinas
(1225–1274) and his scholastic realist contemporaries, aware of
Aristotle and his Arabic commentators, also affirmed sphericity.[50]

The scholastics—later medieval philosophers, theologians,
and scientists—were helped by the Arabic translations and
commentaries, but they hardly needed to struggle against a
flat-earth legacy from the early Middle Ages (500–1050). Early
medieval writers often had fuzzy and imprecise impressions of
both Ptolemy and Aristotle and relied more on Pliny, but they
felt (with one exception) little urge to assume flatness.[51] The
two most influential writers on geography were Macrobius (c.
400), a Neoplatonist of uncertain background, and Martianus
Capella (c. 420), whose concept of seven liberal arts, including
astronomy and geometry, became the basis for the medieval
educational curriculum. Martianus says flatly that the earth is
neither flat nor concave, but spherical.[52]

Isidore of Seville (d. 636), the most widely read encyclope-
dist of the early Middle Ages, has often been cited as a "flat-
earther." It is true that some passages of his "Etymologies" can
be interpreted either way, but the ambiguity is owing to his rel-
ative lack of concern about the subject. His "Treatise on
Nature" gives an estimate of the earth's circumference, and on
balance Isidore can be said to have believed that the earth was
round.[53]

Vergil of Salzburg, an Irish bishop in eighth-century Aus-
tria, was reprimanded for believing in the antipodes.[54] This has

led some modern writers to confuse the question of the antipodes with that of the sphericity of the earth, and this became an important element in the Flat Error. In the ancient and medieval world the term "antipodes" may mean lands on the opposite side of the planet or, more commonly, *human inhabitants* of lands on the other side of the planet. Several varieties of view on the antipodes existed, some placing them in the southern hemisphere, others in the northern hemisphere opposite the known world.

To distinguish, it will help to call the inhabitants "antipodeans." Christian doctrine affirmed that all humans must be of one origin, descended from Adam and Eve and redeemable by Christ, "the second Adam." The Bible was silent as to whether antipodeans existed, but natural philosophy had demonstrated that if they did, they could have no connection with the known part of the globe, either because the sea was too wide to sail across or because the equatorial zones were too hot to sail through. There could be no genetic connection between the antipodeans and us. Therefore any alleged antipodeans could not be descended from Adam and therefore could not exist. Albertus Magnus, Roger Bacon, and some other philosophers noted that there was no proof that the ocean was unnavigable, but objections to antipodeans were still being heard as late as Zacharia Lilio in 1496. At any rate, Vergil of Salzburg was reproved (not burnt, as some later historians said) for believing in antipodeans, not for believing in sphericity.

Bede (673–735), the great historian and natural scientist of the early Middle Ages, affirmed that the earth is at the center of a spherical cosmos; the earth is a globe that can be called a perfect sphere because the surface irregularities of mountains and valleys are so small in comparison to its vast size. Bede specifies that the earth is "round" *not* in the sense of "circular" but in the sense of a ball. In the ninth century, the greatest philosopher of the early Middle Ages, John Scottus Eriugena, was equally firm on the subject.[55]

Raban Maur (776–856), like Isidore, was ambiguous and unclear; he made an ill-advised attempt at a mathematical reconciliation between biblical texts on "the corners of the earth" and the scientific knowledge of its circularity or sphericity. Sometimes, using the word *rota,* "wheel," he seems to imply a disc, but in other passages he is clear that the earth is a "globe."[56] A pictorial demonstration of the round earth in the early Middle Ages is in the portraits of kings holding the symbols of their power. One standard item of regalia is the royal "orb," which the king holds in his hand. It is a golden ball representing the earth, surmounted by a cross indicating Christ's sovereignty over the earth; the king holds it because Christ has entrusted its worldly governance to the monarch. St. John Damascene (675–749) opens the door backward into the earliest period of Christian thought (50–500) by taking a view typical of many of the earlier church fathers, whose influence formed the millennium of thought that followed. Damascene maintained that the shape of the heavens and the earth are irrelevant to the real business of being a Christian, which is moral and spiritual, not philosophical. To Damascene, geographical knowledge was a useless vanity, but if the philosophers show the earth to be a globe, let it be. Damascene followed Basil of Caesarea (330–379), one of the great figures in Eastern Orthodox theology. Basil explained that the earth is at the center of the universe, and the mass of the cosmos presses in on the earth's center from all sides. It follows from this that the earth is probably a sphere, and philosophers have estimated its circumference, but Basil tells his monastic audience that if they cannot follow the logic, they have no need to; they can simply pray and thank God for creation, whatever its shape.[57]

St. Augustine (354–430) took a similar view. The fathers held the Bible to be the highest textual authority, inspired by God, infinitely above any of the writings of secular philosophers. But unlike some modern Christians, few of them took the Bible as a guide to scientific truth. During the Middle Ages, when biblical statements seemed to contradict empirical evidence, they were usually taken allegorically and the empirical evidence accepted as the scientific statement.[58]

It is impossible to be clear as to what the various biblical authors meant by their occasional cosmological references; the books of the Bible, written over a period of more than a thousand years, contain no coherent astronomical or geographical viewpoint. There was and is no "biblical view" of geography. What *can* be known is how the church fathers understood the Bible. The Bible that they used consisted of the New Testament, composed in Greek over the years c. A.D. 50–100, and the Old Testament (and Apocrypha), composed in Hebrew from c. 1000 B.C. to 150 B.C. Those fathers who knew Greek used the Greek New Testament and one or another variety of the Greek Septuagint translation of the Old Testament (third and second centuries B.C.). Others used Latin translations, the most influential being the "Vulgate" Bible of St. Jerome.

One of the crucial passages is Psalm 104:2-3, which thus addresses God: "You stretch out the heavens like a skin (or tent) and build your palace on the waters above; using the clouds as your chariot, you advance on the wings of the wind." The fathers were aware that anyone insisting that this means that the heavens resemble a tent physically must also be prepared to argue that God lives in a physical palace on the water and drives an actual chariot.[59]

In his *Literal Meaning of Genesis,* Augustine observes that the Bible contains no clear description of the physical shape and size of the earth or the universe. Accordingly he warns Christians not to make fools of themselves by snatching isolated texts from the Scriptures and using them against the pagan philosophers. Fools who ascribe their own silly views to the Bible will only make pagans contemptuous of Christians and their Scriptures. Since the Bible does not tell us the shape of the earth, it is irrelevant to our salvation, and discussing it is idle. Nonetheless, it is a matter for natural investigation. So, continues Augustine, precisely because the Bible does not answer the question, we should be open to the evidence that the philosophers present. It matters little to us, but if they can demonstrate that it is a sphere, we may take it to be a sphere. Augustine makes a particular point of refuting Christians who use the skins or tents of Psalms, Isaiah, Job, or Amos to argue against sphericity.[60] We must take them as metaphors. What the sacred writers intend by "skin" or "tent" is a moral, not a geographical, statement. As an unnecessary concession, Augustine goes on to say that there are ways of reconciling them with sphericity even if taken as geographical statements, for the hemisphere of the sky above our heads is in the *shape* of a vault, and a skin may be stretched into the shape of a sphere, as with a leather ball. But Augustine does not dwell on such games. For him the point is that Scripture can be read in many ways, and statements couched in physical terms may often be taken allegorically or morally instead of physically.[61]

In *The City of God* Augustine distinguishes clearly between antipodes and sphericity. It seems that the earth is round, he says, but even if there is land on the opposite side, no one could ever have crossed the huge expanse of ocean to settle it.[62]

The fathers, who claimed the divine inspiration of the Bible, essentially took one of two views toward the tradition of pagan learning that surrounded them. Either they attempted to synthesize the Bible and philosophy, as Augustine did; or they attacked the philosophers, sometimes ignoring Augustine's appeal for caution. Most of the fathers took the former view and settled down with sphericity. Ambrose described the earth as a sphere suspended in the void, its weight evenly balanced on every side.[63]

But a few real flat-earthers did exist. Lactantius (c. 265–345) and Cosmas Indicopleustes (c. 540) are discussed in chapter 3 as the chief scapegoats of the nineteenth century. Lactantius seems to have denied roundness as part of denying the antipodes, and Cosmas blundered into constructing a physical cosmology on the basis of the Bible. Theodore of Mopsuestia (c. 350–430) may also have argued for a flat earth, although the evidence is indirect.[64] The views of Diodore of Tarsus (d. 394) on the subject are also known only indirectly; in the ninth century Photius of Constantinople attacked Diodore's treatise "Against Fate" for denying the sphericity of both the earth and the heavens in favor of tents and vaults.[65] The "Homilies on the Creation of the World" by Severian, Bishop of Gabala (c. 380), are direct without a doubt. Severian says that God did not make the sky a sphere, as the Greek philosophers say. He said that Christians believe that the sky is a tent or a vault. The sun does not go under the earth at night, but rather goes to the far north, where its light is hidden from us by the bulge of the waters.[66]

The Greeks' knowledge of the earth's roundness has never been disputed by any serious writers.[67] The earliest Greek philosophers are vague, but "after the fifth century B.C. no Greek writer of any repute" thought of the earth as anything but round.[68] The only exceptions are the atomists Leucippus and Democritus, who seem to have imagined a flat disc surrounded by air. Pythagoras (c. 530 B.C.), Parmenides (c. 480 B.C.), Eudoxus (c. 375 B.C.), Plato (c. 428–348 B.C.), Aristotle (384–322 B.C.), Euclid (c. 300 B.C.), Aristarchus (c. 310–230 B.C.), and Archimedes (287–212 B.C.) all took the round view.[69]

Aristotle's concept became a traditional standard: the earth was an immobile sphere at the center of the universe, with the heavenly bodies moving around it in perfect, concentric spheres. The center of the earth's sphere was thus the center of the cosmos. The earth must be a sphere because the sphere is the perfect shape; because all earthy matter is pulled downward by natural motion toward a central point; because only a sphere includes the maximum volume of evenly distributed matter around the center; because mathematical symmetry requires that the earth be spherical like the heavens. As Kuhn put it, "If particles are moving from all sides alike to one point, the center, the resulting mass must be similar on all sides; for if an equal quantity is added all round, the extremity must be at a constant distance from the center. Such a shape is a sphere." Also, since the inclination of all mass is to press on other mass as far as it can, all mass will press to the center, "and the impulsion of the less heavy by the heavier persists to that point."[70]

Aristotle saw that the evidence for the earth's sphericity lies in the spherical appearance of the heavens, in the limitation of our view over the sea by the curvature of the earth, in the fact that we see the stars differently depending on our latitude, in the perfect motion of the stars, which implies that they move on a perfect sphere, in that the hull of a ship disappears from our eyes before the mast does, in that the higher one's elevation the farther one can see, and in that eclipses of the moon are caused by the shadow of the spherical earth.

Following Aristotle, Eratosthenes (276–195 B.C.), librarian of Alexandria, measured the earth's circumference using trigonometry on data obtained from observations of the sun's declination at different latitudes (Alexandria and Aswan [Syene]). Eratosthenes suggested that a map of the world would be in the shape of an oblong from Gibraltar to India in the long dimension and from the arctic to the Sahara in the short dimension. But by "world" Eratosthenes had in mind the known world, the inhabited part of the planet, which he estimated to occupy approximately one of its quarters.[71]

In the Hellenistic and Roman world of the last few centuries B.C., such maps, along with three-dimensional globes, "were used in schools and sometimes displayed in public places."[72] Under the Roman Empire, most of the good geographical work continued to be done by Greeks, such as Strabo (born c. 63 B.C.) and Crates of Mallos (c. 150 B.C.), who constructed a terrestrial globe in Rome more than 3 meters in diameter; it was his view that there were continents in each of the four quadrants ("corners") of the earth, which was divided by two impassable oceans, one running north and south and the other east and west. Only one continent — our oikoumene, or known world — was inhabited.[73]

Claudius Ptolemy (A.D. 90–168) systematized the works of his predecessors and constructed an accurate map of the known world. His great achievement was to enter detailed information about the known world onto a map projected from a sphere onto a flat surface. Ptolemy's work later became the basis for the revival of scientific geography early in the fifteenth century.

He criticized and corrected the work of Marinus of Tyre (c. A.D. 100), arguing against Marinus's and Erastosthenes' rectangular projections in favor of one contracting toward the pole and expanding at the equator. These are projections for maps, *not* geometrical descriptions. Columbus would prefer the tradition of Marinus as interpreted by D'Ailly, because Marinus's ocean was much smaller than Ptolemy's.[74] Ptolemy was unfortunately soon forgotten in the West until the twelfth century, so the writers of the Roman Empire who had the most influence for the next millennium were the less exact Pomponius Mela (c. 40) and Pliny (23–79).[75]

In the first fifteen centuries of the Christian era, five writers seem to have denied the globe, and a few others were ambiguous and uninterested in the question. But nearly unanimous scholarly opinion pronounced the earth spherical, and by the fifteenth century all doubt had disappeared. There was no "Great Interruption" in this era.[76] So what or who led to the Flat Error?

CHAPTER THREE

Flattening the Globe

Nineteenth- and twentieth-century writers flattened the medieval globe.[77] Daniel Boorstin paints a pathetic picture of the brave mariners of the fifteenth century struggling valiantly against the darkness. In their efforts to navigate accurately, they "did not find much help in Cosmas Indicopleustes' neat box of the universe. . . . The outlines of the seacoast . . . could not be modified or ignored by what was written in Isidore of Seville or even in Saint Augustine. . . . The schematic Christian T-O map was little use to Europeans seeking an eastward sea passage to the Indies."[78] In fact, Cosmas Indicopleustes was unknown in the fifteenth century; Isidore and Augustine had nothing to say about the outlines of the coast; and the T-O maps were never intended for navigation.

The untruth of the Flat Error lies in its incoherence as well as in its violation of facts. First there is the flat-out Flat Error that *never* before Columbus did anyone know that the world was round. This dismisses the careful calculations of the Greek geographers along with their medieval successors; it makes Aristotle, the most eloquent of round-earthers, and Ptolemy, the most accurate, into flat-earthers.

Another crude form of the Flat Error is the lurid embellishment that sailors feared that they would plunge off the edge of the flat earth if they voyaged too far out into the ocean. The falling-off-the-edge fallacy was popularized by Andrew Dickson White, who wrote in 1896:

> Many a bold navigator, who was quite ready to brave pirates and tempests, trembled at the thought of tumbling with his ship into one of the openings into hell which a widespread belief placed in the Atlantic at some unknown distance from Europe. This terror among sailors was one of the main obstacles in the great voyage of Columbus.[79]

The Flat Error later combined openings into hell with the edge of the earth and simple sailors with experienced navigators.

Another version of the Error is that the ancient Greeks may have known that the world was round, but the knowledge was lost (or suppressed) in medieval darkness. According to this argument, the Middle Ages were a dark period for the development of science in Europe. At best, scholars made accurate but sterile copies of the works of the ancients, rejecting anything that did not conform with the dogmas of the Church. Such an intellectual environment stifled any development of scientific analysis. Concepts of the world that had been developed in ancient times were reshaped to conform to the teaching of the Church. The earth became a flat disc with Jerusalem at its center.[80]

This line of thought, presented in 1988, represents no advance in knowledge from the following statement, made sixty years earlier:

> The maps of Ptolemy . . . were forgotten in the West for a thousand years, and replaced by imaginary constructions based on the supposed teachings of Holy Writ. The sphericity of the earth was, in fact, formally denied by the Church, and the mind of Western man, so far as it moved in this matter at all, moved back to the old confused notion of a modulated "flatland," with the kingdoms of the world surrounding Jerusalem, the divinely chosen centre of the terrestrial disk.[81]

Many inconsistent varieties of this version exist: The knowledge was lost in the first century A.D., or the second, or the fifth, or the sixth, or the seventh; and on the other end it was lost until the fifteenth century, or the twelfth, or the eighth. The mildest variety, therefore, posits only a few years of darkness from the flattening of the Greek earth to the rounding of the modern one.

Still another version is that almost everyone always believed the earth was flat, but in the darkness had shone a few, scattered lamps, held by Aristotle and Ptolemy and Bacon and Toscanelli. "A few bold thinkers had long believed that the earth was a globe."[82]

The growth of the Error was not steady. In the mid-nineteenth century some specialists remained cautious and accurate. Joachim Lelewel, for example, explained that medieval mapmakers often represented the *inhabitable* world, not the entire earth, as rectangular.[83] The schoolbooks of the nineteenth century are inconsistent, but show an increasing tendency over the century to the Flat Error, a tendency that becomes especially pronounced from the 1870s onward as textbook authors engaged in the evolutionary fray and became more subject to pragmatist influence.[84] Earlier in the century the dominant force behind the Error was middle-class Enlightenment anticlericalism in Europe and "Know-Nothing" anticatholicism in these United States. The origin of the Error resides in these milieus.

Throughout the nineteenth century, middle-class liberal progressives projected their own ideals upon heroes of the past, among them "Columbus, [who] from that justness of mind and reasoning which mathematical knowledge gives, calculated very justly."[85] The image of Columbus as the clear-headed rationalist is at odds with both the original sources and the judgment of his most recent and definitive biographers. This Columbus existed only in the minds of amiable progressives whose disdain for the Catholic Revival and the Romantics of the early nineteenth century colored the way they viewed the Middle Ages.[86] To the political and ecclesiastical liberals, Romanticism and Catholicism (in reality seldom allies) were twin obstacles to progress. "In discarding medieval naivete and superstition . . . men looked to the guidance of Greek and Roman thinkers, and called up the spirit of the ancient world to exorcise the ghosts of the dark ages."[87] This fit their image of Columbus.

Philosophers of progress such as Hegel (1770–1831) wrote about the infinite falsehood constituting the life and spirit of the Middle Ages. Romantic populists such as Jules Michelet attacked the clergy and the aristocracy as relics of the medieval mind. For Michelet the age of feudalism and scholasticism was a time of gathering darkness; the scholastics were somehow at one and the same time "valiant athletes of stupidity" and "trembling with timidity." Columbus, these writers said, defied them and discovered the earth as Copernicus would discover the heavens.[88]

Auguste Comte (1798–1857) laid the philosophical basis for positivism with the argument that the history of humanity shows an unsteady but definite progress from reliance on magic, then religion, then philosophy, then natural science. A few definitions are necessary for clarity and precision. There is a spectrum of beliefs held by those who adopt a generally "scientific worldview." Some believe that there is no knowledge outside human constructs of it. Some maintain that science is only one of a number of roads to knowledge. Some believe that external reality exists and that science is making successively more exact approximations to truth about that reality without ever (or at least probably ever) coming to truth itself. Some maintain that science can and does express truth about the external world. And some (a decreasing number) maintain that science tells *the* truth, the *only* truth about the external world. The belief that science expresses the truth, or at least some truth, about the external world I call "scientific realism." The view that science is approaching the truth by successive approximations I call positivism. In common usage in the nineteenth and twentieth centuries, the terms scientific realism and positivism are often exchanged and used loosely, and in fact some writers did not distinguish between them. Positivism extends beyond natural science, too; historical positivism, for example, is the view that history advances toward truth about the human past in successive approximations. There is no one common term to embrace both scientific realists and positivists, so for the purpose of this book I will call both "progressivists."

Progressivists did not choose to understand other societies in those societies' terms, but, rather, chose to hold them to the standards of the nineteenth-century scientific method. By making that method the criterion of all truth and goodness, the progressivists necessarily ruled out other worldviews as false and bad. By the nineteenth century their victory was so complete that other views now seemed merely irrational, superstitious, trivial.

The progressivists succeeded, mainly in the half century between 1870 and 1920, in establishing the Flat Error firmly in the modern mind. As late as 1867 a rationalist historian such as W.E.H. Lecky could point to the church fathers' objections against antipodeans and to the bizarre ideas of Cosmas Indicopleustes without claiming that the fathers believed in a flat earth. Such a polemical rationalist and anticlerical as Charles Kingsley could refrain from the Error. Lecky and Kingsley were intent on attacking medieval philosophy — scholasticism — on the grounds that it dogmatically conformed to Aristotle, they knew very well that Aristotle's earth was round, and they knew that it followed logically that they could not accuse the scholastics of being flat-earthers.[89]

The ground was prepared for the alleged "warfare between science and religion" suggested by William Whewell (1794–1866), Vice-Chancellor of Cambridge University and priest of the Church of England. Whewell took his doctorate in Divinity when that degree was standard and normal for a learned man, but his interests were science and mathematics (and to some degree poetry) rather than religion. "His sermons do not exhibit any special theological learning, and it is curious that . . . he should have been so little attracted by divinity."[90] His *History of the Inductive Sciences,* first published in 1837, became the standard text in the history of science for half a century. A liberal progressive whose imperious character brooked no nonsense, Whewell spoke of "the Indistinctness of Ideas, the Commentatorial Spirit, the Dogmatism, and the mysticism of the Middle Ages." In later editions Whewell pointed to the culprits Lactantius and Cosmas Indicopleustes as evidence of a medieval belief in a flat earth, and virtually every subsequent historian imitated him — they could find few other examples.[91]

Lactantius (c. 245–325) was born and reared in Africa as a pagan. A professional rhetorician, he converted to Christianity and wrote a number of books defending his new faith. But his views eventually led to his works being condemned as heretical after his death. He maintained, for example, that God wills evil as a logical necessity and that Christ and Satan are metaphorical twins, two angels, two spirits, one good and one evil, both created by God.[92] The irony is that after being under some suspicion through the Middle Ages, Lactantius was revived by the Humanists of the Renaissance as a model of excellent Latin style. Lactantius, revolting against his own pagan upbringing, rejected the teachings of the Greek philosophers on every point he could. The philosophers argue for sphericity, he wrote, but there is no evidence to support their view that the earth is round, and as the Bible is not clear on the subject, it is unimportant. In this view, he was similar to Augustine and Basil. But unfortunately he went on, as his detractors did seventeen-hundred years later, to tie the question of roundness to that of the antipodes. Is there anyone so silly, he demanded, as to believe that there are humans on the other side of the earth, with their feet above their heads, where crops and trees grow upside down, and rain and snow fall upward and the sky is lower than the ground? From Lactantius's angle of vision, Christians were faced with two competing approaches to truth: one based on the authority of the revealed Scriptures and the other based on the authority of philosophical logic. It was coherent for Lactantius to believe that revelation must be prior to any human system of thought; that is central to a coherent Christian worldview. However, his mistake lay in trying to force the philosophers into the biblical mode, failing to distinguish, as Augustine and Chrysostom had, between two *kinds* of statements, the scientific and the revealed, which need not be reconciled in one system. At any rate, Lactantius was not widely heeded.

The other villain for the progressivists was from the Greek East: Cosmas Indicopleustes. Cosmas wrote a "Christian Topography" (547–549), in which he argued that the cosmos was a huge, rectangular, vaulted arch with the earth as a flat floor. Cosmas drew upon a misapprehension of both the Bible and the pagan philosophers. He chose naively to take as science the poetic biblical passages about the earth having ends and four corners and the sky being spread above it like a tent or a vault.[93] Like Lactantius, Cosmas courted difficulty by trying to reconcile biblical metaphor and philosophical logic.[94] He also misinterpreted the scientific description of the world as being rectangular and longer East–West than North–South. His confusion was based upon the longstanding ambiguity as to the meaning of the term "world." Eratosthenes and Strabo had drawn rectangular maps to represent the known world, which they knew occupied a portion of the surface of the spherical earth: their maps were attempts at projection. Cosmas took such views as implying a physically flat, oblong earth.[95]

Cosmas argued against the sphericity of heaven and earth and the existence of the antipodes. The New Testament Epistle to the Hebrews 9:1-5, following the Book of Exodus, calls the Tabernacle of Moses *to hagion kosmikon*, literally, "the cosmic holy thing." A modern translation is "a sanctuary on this earth," but Cosmas took it to mean that the earth had the same shape as the Tabernacle. If the Tabernacle of Moses is constructed in imitation of the shape of the world, then it follows that the world must be in the shape of the Tabernacle. Cosmas saw the enclosed vault of the sky as the Tabernacle itself and the earth

as the flat table on which the "showbread" or "loaves of presen-
tation" were placed. As the table was oblong, the earth must be
oblong as well. Cosmas derived the image from the influential
church father Origen of Alexandria (185–251), whose method
of interpreting Scripture was strongly allegorical. Origen understood such a statement as Hebrews chapter 9 as metaphor,
but Cosmas did not grasp the refinement.[96]

Cosmas knew about the Aristotelian view of a round earth
surrounded by concentric spheres but rejected it. He believed
that night is caused by the sun's passing behind a huge mountain in the far north.[97] Cosmas's scheme is bizarre, but modern
anthropologists and historians have shown that if anything in
another culture strikes us as strange, we should be alert to levels
of understanding that we are not immediately grasping. What
did Cosmas intend with such a system? It appears that he did
not intend to furnish a physical geography, much less a practical
guide to travel. He wanted, like Dante later, to convey the essential meaning of a cosmos whose innermost sense is moral
and spiritual. For Cosmas the physical universe was primarily a
metaphor for the spiritual cosmos. It mattered little to him
whether the physical cosmos he designed to illustrate his point
was geographically valid. Unfortunately, his emphasis upon the
physical details of the system led him into trouble.[98] Unlike
Dante's, his system was muddled and cumbersome.

But the influence of Cosmas's blundered effort on the Middle
Ages was virtually nil. In Greek only three reasonably full
manuscripts of Cosmas exist from the Middle Ages, with five or
six substantial fragments.[99] Cosmas was roundly attacked in his
own time by John Philoponus (490–570). Philoponus, striving
for a reconciliation of philosophy and theology, insisted (like
almost all the fathers) that Christians not make statements
about the physical cosmos that were contradictory to reason
and observation and thus made Christianity look foolish in the
eyes of the educated pagans.[100] After Philoponus, Cosmas was
ignored until the ninth century, when the Patriarch Photius of
Constantinople again dismissed his views. In Latin, no medie-

val text of Cosmas exists at all. The *first* translation of Cosmas
into Latin, his very first introduction into western Europe, was
not until 1706.[101] He had absolutely no influence on medieval
western thought.

The standard modern history text of cartography observes:

> Many general histories devote undue consideration to the con-
> cept of a flat, rectangular four-cornered earth with a vaulted
> heaven. . . . It is important to realize that Cosmas's text . . . was
> not thought worthy of mention by medieval commentators.[102]

But when Cosmas was translated into English in 1897, he appeared not only as a fool but as typical of medieval foolish-
ness.[103] A distinguished historian in 1926 claimed that Cosmas
"had great popularity among even the educated till the twelfth
[century]." And a standard book on geography in 1938 merely
conceded that "Cosmas and the other supporters of the flat
earth theory did not have it all their own way — even in the Dark
Ages."[104]

Why make Lactantius and Cosmas villains? They were convenient symbols to be used as weapons against the anti-
Darwinists. By the 1870s the relationship between science and
theology was beginning to be described in military metaphors.
The philosophes (the propagandists of the Enlightenment),
particularly Hume, had planted a seed by implying that the
scientific and Christian views were in conflict. Auguste Comte
(1798–1857) had argued that humanity was laboriously struggling upward toward the reign of science; his followers advanced the corollary that anything impeding the coming of the
kingdom of science was retrograde. Their value system perceived the movement toward science as "good," so that anything
blocking movement in that direction was "evil."

It was not logically necessary for religion (which in their context meant Christianity) to be "evil," since Christianity had
through the ages usually promoted and sponsored science. Past

theologians had recognized that religion and science are two divergent worldviews, with different roots, and they should not be confounded. Religion's roots are in the poetic, the nonrational (not "irrational") preconscious; science's in analytical reason.[105] But by 1870 the Catholic Church had, under Pius IX (1846–1878), declared itself hostile to modern liberalism; and theological conservatism was rising in many segments of Protestantism as well. Interpreting the contemporary situation as reflecting the *longue durée* (long run) of the relationship between science and religion, the progressivists declared it a war.

The military metaphor was an enormous success. It got its tenacious grip on intellect during the period 1870-1910 when images of war dominated Western society. Germany had just created a new empire and defeated France; Britain would go to war with the Boers, and the United States with Spain. The whole age echoed gunfire: the Salvation Army; the Church Militant; the Battle Hymn of the Republic; Onward Christian Soldiers; jingoism; the naval competition between Germany and Britain; the building of colonial empires. The "Social Darwinists" were arguing that Europe's military superiority proved that it was destined to rule the world. The military metaphor was striking, colorful, well-timed, and so effective a propaganda tool that today it is still common to think of science and religion as being in armed conflict.

The opening barrage of the war came from John W. Draper.[106] Draper (1811–1882) came from a religious family; his father was an itinerant Methodist preacher, and at the age of eleven John was sent to a Methodist school. However much he rejected these origins later, he retained the Methodist's optimistic belief that progress can be won through hard work. He studied briefly at University College London, where he was exposed to positivism and began to translate his progressive faith in religion into a progressive faith in science. After his father's death, he emigrated in 1832 with his mother, wife, and sisters to the United States, studied medicine at Pennsylvania, and became professor of chemistry and biology at New York University and eventually head of the medical school.

He governed his family's marriages, money, and even leisure. On matters of religion he brooked no opposition. When his sister Elizabeth's son William died at the age of eight, she put the boy's prayer book on Draper's breakfast plate. It was a challenge that her brother accepted by driving her from the house; she became a Catholic convert and remained alienated from the family.

In 1860, after presenting evolutionary views in a paper read to the British Association, Draper was attacked by Bishop Wilberforce, whose expressed intention was to "smash Darwin," and then defended by Thomas Huxley in a crushing counterattack. The confrontation encouraged Draper to believe that religion and science were at war.[107] By 1860 he had already completed his *History of the Intellectual Development of Europe,* although it was not published until 1862 owing to the U.S. Civil War, and the first edition shows a more irenic spirit than his later work. It argued that humanity was making slow but steady progress and that the growth of science was in the best interests of a healthy Christianity. Indeed, Europe's alleged Enlightenment as opposed to the decadence of China, Draper explained, may be traced to the benevolent influence of Christianity. But Christianity would have to accept as its basis science in place of revelation. The book denounced the fathers and the scholastics for subordinating science to the Bible.[108]

The British Association meeting, the increasing intractability of Protestantism to the theory of evolution, and especially the escalating hostility of the papacy to liberal thought, convinced Draper during the 1860s that Christianity — or at least Roman Catholicism — would never give up its epistemological basis in Scripture and tradition and would be an obstacle rather than an aid to progress, which he defined as the advance of science and technology. In 1873 he began a new book, *The History of the Conflict between Religion and Science,* largely a popular condensation of his earlier work with a few additions, but in tone and attitude combining the Enlightenment skepticism of Gibbon and the positivism of Comte with the political liberal's faith in the advance of society. "For his own taste he had made a gratifying whole of science and liberalism."[109] The *History of the Conflict* is of immense importance, because it was the first instance that an influential figure had explicitly declared that science and religion were at war, and it succeeded as few books ever do. It fixed in the educated mind the idea that "science" stood for freedom and progress against the superstition and repression of "religion." Its viewpoint became conventional wisdom.

There was some hope, Draper felt, that science could live with Protestantism, because liberal Protestantism was yielding its moral authority to the secular state and its epistemological basis to science. But science could never live with Catholicism, which under Pius IX condemned liberal progressivism in the "Syllabus of Errors," opposed the union of Italy into a secular state, and declared the pope's infallibility. The pope, as Draper saw it, was clinging to his eroding power by attempting to quash freedom of thought. Draper saw the secular national state as the protector and steward of liberal progress, and he admired Bismarck's "Cultural War" (*Kulturkampf*) against the church in Germany. This was also the period when American Know-Nothing hatred of Catholicism was being stoked by waves of Irish and Italian immigrants who, American Protestants and secularists believed, threatened to divide the nation or even bring it under papal tyranny.

It was also the heyday of the *leyenda negra,* or "Black Legend of Spain," which perceived Spanish Catholicism of the sixteenth and seventeenth centuries to be the evil force behind Bloody Mary, the Armada, and the "Inquisition," a force dedicated to the destruction of decent (especially Anglo) Protestantism.[110] The Black Legend began in England under Elizabeth I (1558–1603), when parts of Bartolomé de las Casas were translated into English. Las Casas had favored lenient treatment of the Amerindians under Spanish rule and as a result had in his works condemned the Spanish exploiters. These passages were eagerly seized upon by the English (and the Dutch and other Protestant powers) to prove the evil of the Spanish Catholics. It

was ironic, of course, since the English were much more ruth-
less in exterminating the Indians than the Catholic Spanish or
Portuguese, but again the fallacy fit the political programs of
the Protestant powers and Protestant popular prejudice.

Draper wrote that the Catholic Church and science are "absolutely incompatible; they cannot exist together; one must
yield to the other; mankind must make its choice — it cannot
have both."[111]

When and where had Christianity gone wrong? Draper's
new book offered two answers:

> The antagonism we thus witness between Religion and Science is
> the continuation of the struggle that commenced when Chris-
> tianity began to attain political power. A divine revelation must
> necessarily be intolerant of contradiction; it must repudiate all
> improvement in itself, and view with disdain that arising from
> the progressive intellectual development of man. . . . The his-
> tory of Science is not a mere record of isolated discoveries; it is a
> narrative of the conflict of two contending powers, the expansive
> force of the human intellect on one side, and the compression
> arising from traditionary [sic] faith and human interests on the
> other. . . . Faith is in its nature unchangeable, stationary; Sci-
> ence is in its nature progressive; and eventually a divergence be-
> tween them, impossible to conceal, must take place. [It is the
> duty of the educated to take a stand, for] when the old mytholog-
> ical religion of Europe broke down under the weight of its own
> inconsistencies, neither the Roman emperors nor the philoso-
> phers of those times did any thing [sic] adequate for the guidance
> of public opinion. They left religious affairs to take their chance,
> and accordingly those affairs fell into the hands of ignorant and
> infuriated ecclesiastics, parasites, eunuchs, and slaves.[112]

One suggestion implicit here is that Christianity went wrong by
assuming political power. Draper explained that this happened
in fourth-century Rome with the conversion of Constantine to
Christianity and developed over the centuries into nineteenth-

century monarchical papalism. The other suggestion is that Christianity was inherently and absolutely wrong from the outset in basing itself upon divine revelation. There was no comfort in his words to Protestants, though some nurtured a fond hope of distancing themselves from the ignorant ecclesiastics, parasites, eunuchs, and slaves in the Vatican, whose hands "have been steeped in blood."[113] Soon, however, Protestantism was to share the fate of Catholicism in being declared an obstacle to Progress.

Draper was right that the epistemological bases of science and religion are different, but in projecting his condemnation backward on nineteen centuries of Christianity, he saw the whole religion in the image of Pius IX. Draper's description of the church fathers' cosmological views failed even as caricature. He despised St. Augustine particularly, attributing to him views more appropriate to a dim nineteenth-century nonconformist preacher. "No one did more than this Father to bring science and religion into antagonism; it was mainly he who diverted the Bible from its true office — a guide to the purity of life — and placed it in the perilous position of being the arbiter of human knowledge, an audacious tyranny over the mind of man." In their ignorance the fathers "saw in the Almighty, the Eternal, only a gigantic man."[114] They believed that the Bible was to be taken as scientific truth, an allegation Draper of course extended to the Middle Ages. In the same sentence that he claimed everyone knew the sphericity of the planet, he said that the dominant scholasticism of the universities rejected it. "The writings of the Mohammedan astronomers and philosophers had given currency to that doctrine [of a spherical earth] throughout western Europe, but, as might be expected, it was received with disfavor by theologians."[115] Draper did not explain how, if the scholastics, the intellectual leaders of the time, had rejected it, it could have been generally received. He said that Columbus was attacked at Salamanca by fanatical pedants led by the alleged "Grand Cardinal of Spain," hurling arguments drawn from "St. Chrysostom and St. Augustine, St. Jerome . . . St. Basil and St. Ambrose."[116] Draper's *Conflict* was the best selling volume of the International Scientific Series; in the United States it had fifty printings in fifty years, in the United Kingdom twenty-one in fifteen years; and it was translated worldwide.[117]

Draper might not have been so successful had it not been for the emergence of the controversy over evolution and the "descent of man." This controversy seemed to Draper and his colleagues to be another major battle in the supposedly ancient "war between religion and science." The symbolic beginning of this battle was the confrontation in 1860 between Wilberforce and Huxley. For nearly a century the hostilities continued, and Draper's military metaphor took hold in the popular imagination. Christian extremists insisted that Biblical texts that were intended as myth or poetry be taken as science. Polemicists on the "science" side oddly agreed with the religious extremists that the Biblical texts were intended as science, but used this argument to declare the Bible to be bad science. Neither side grasped that religion and natural science were simply two different ways of thinking, two epistemological "languages" that could not readily be translated into one another.

Zealous in protecting biological and geographical facts, the progressivist warriors projected their own methodological error onto the fathers and scholastics, blaming them for suppressing truth in order to support a dogmatic system. The progressivists in the trenches drew upon Draper in their schoolbooks:

> The sphericity of the earth was a doctrine held by many at that day [Columbus's]; but the theory was not in harmony with the religious ideas of the time, and so it was not prudent for one to publish openly one's belief in the notion.[118]

In higher academic ranks Draper's flag was carried deeper into enemy territory by Andrew Dickson White (1832–1918).[119] Like Draper, White rebelled against his upbringing. His family were high-church Episcopalians who sent him to a religious boarding school that he hated. When he rose to educational prominence, he faced down strong religious opposition in founding Cornell University (1868) as the first determinedly and explicitly secular university in the United States. He became president of Cornell at the age of 33. Whereas Draper's animosity was focused on Catholics, White's ire was turned against Protestants as well, for it was Protestants who obstructed his work as president of the university. White was also troubled by the virulence of American anticatholicism as symbolized by the Ku Klux Klan, and he understood that it was artificial historically to separate Catholicism from Christianity in general.

On December 18, 1869, White delivered a fiery sermon in defense of science against the anti-Darwinists, a lecture published in full in the *New York Daily Tribune* the following day. Widely publicized, this material appeared in 1876 in articles in the United Kingdom and the United States (including *Popular Science*), and as a pamphlet, under the title "The Warfare of Science," primarily aimed at pious New Yorkers opposing the creation of a secular university at Cornell. White gradually "narrowed the focus of his attack: from 'religion' in 1869, to 'ecclesiasticism' in 1876, when he published a little book entitled *The Warfare of Science,* and finally to 'dogmatic theology' in 1896, when he brought out his fully documented, two-volume *History of the Warfare of Science with Theology in Christendom.*" By 1896 he had shifted his views to recognize the value of *religion,* as opposed to *theology,* which, he said, "smothered" truth.[120]

> It is only just to make a distinction here between the religious and the theological spirit . . . that tendency to dogmatism which has shown itself in all ages the deadly foe not only of scientific inquiry but of the higher religious spirit itself.[121]

White's efforts to construct a new Christianity based on that "higher religious spirit" were doomed, for scientific realists insisted that all truth was scientific and that there was no room for revelation, while traditional Christians insisted that if Scripture and tradition were dismissed, Christianity was left with no intellectual basis. By the time White reinforced Draper and Whewell, the Flat Error had grown to a stature that entirely dwarfed the historical reality.

Scientific realists saw the Flat Error as a powerful weapon. If Christians had for centuries insisted that the earth was flat against clear and available evidence, they must be not only enemies of scientific truth, but contemptible and pitiful enemies. The Error, which had existed in seed from the time of Copernicus and had been planted by Irving and Letronne in the nineteenth century (see chapter 4), was now watered by the progressivists into lush and tangled undergrowth. The Error was thus subsumed in a much larger controversy — the alleged war between science and religion.

Meanwhile the nature of progressivism had changed. After about 1870, Enlightenment "secular humanism" was gradually replaced by pragmatism, especially as put forward by William James. Although Enlightenment rationalism differed strongly from Christian rationalism, both shared the belief that the use of reason could lead us to, or at least toward, the truth. Pragmatism was a radical break with the rational tradition. It was no longer truth that was sought but "what worked" in a given problem or field. The result was a movement toward solipsism, subjectivism, and relativism. True relativism is compatible with "progress" in the solving of certain individual problems defined within the parameters of a "game," but it is entirely incompatible with the idea of progress in general, because by definition there is no universal goal — truth or otherwise. Oddly, pragmatism nonetheless became linked with progressivism in that it emphasized survival value of the "best" of what we have. The problem was that there was no standard by which "better" or "worse" could be measured. Later, existentialism would try to build human standards from scratch, but the legacy of pragmatism remained strong. In the late nineteenth century and early twentieth century the prevalence of pragmatism predisposed people even more strongly to the notion that medieval, Christian, or other noncurrent-Western views were unworthy of consideration.

White attacked the fathers, although with greater restraint than his predecessors. A scholar where Draper had been a propagandist, White knew that the fathers as a whole approved of sphericity, but his thesis pushed him to minimize this fact: "A few of the larger-minded fathers of the Church . . . were willing to accept this view, but the majority of them took fright at once."[122] He went on to misrepresent St. Basil and St. John Chrysostom as flat-earthers, apparently because he did not read them. He cited as sources only secondary writers who shared his opinions: Kretschmer, Draper, and of course Whewell.[123] The curious result is that White and his colleagues ended by doing what they accused the fathers of, namely, creating a body of false knowledge by consulting one another instead of the evidence. Thus White continues:

[The fathers] were not content with merely opposing what they stigmatized as an old heathen theory; they drew from their Bibles a new Christian theory, to which one Church authority added one idea and another, until it was fully developed.[124]

In fact, as two distinguished current historians of science observe, "The notion that any serious Christian thinker would even have attempted to formulate a world view from the Bible alone is ludicrous."[125]

In defense of what he already assumed to be true, White proceeded illogically:

As to the movement of the sun, there was a citation of various passages in Genesis, mixed with metaphysics in various proportions, and this was thought to give ample proofs that the earth could not be a sphere.[126]

White presented Cosmas Indicopleustes as typical and influential. During the Middle Ages "some of the foremost men in the Church devoted themselves to buttressing [Cosmas] with new texts and throwing about it new networks of theological reasoning." He also lambasted Lactantius, declaring him typical of the "great majority of the early fathers of the Church." Unlike Draper he admitted that Clement of Alexandria, Origen, Ambrose, and Augustine knew about the round earth and that Isidore of Seville in the seventh century and Bede in the eighth defended it, but then he made the odd statement that they went against the dominant theology of a flat earth. Like Draper, White did not explain how Origen and Augustine, two of the most influential fathers, and Isidore and Bede, the two most influential early medieval writers, could be said to be against the "dominant theology" of Lactantius, condemned as a heretic, and of Cosmas, unread and ignored.

White wrote that for the later Middle Ages, "eminent authorities . . . like Albert the Great, St. Thomas Aquinas, Dante, and Vincent of Beauvais, felt obliged to accept the doctrine of the earth's sphericity." White acknowledged the truth that everyone but a few strange people accepted it, yet continued the rhetorical tradition that these were brave individuals struggling against a reactionary flat-earth dogmatism. White said, for example, that Gerbert and Roger Bacon had come close to calculating the circumference of the planet correctly—but that their reward was to be considered sorcerers.[127]

White's Columbus was the brave navigator "at war" with ignorant theologians:

> The warfare of Columbus the world knows well: how the Bishop of Ceuta worsted him in Portugal; how sundry wise men of Spain confronted him with the usual quotations from the Psalms, from St. Paul, and from St. Augustine; how, even after he was triumphant, and after his voyage had greatly strengthened the theory of the earth's sphericity . . . the Church by its highest authority

solemnly stumbled and persisted in going astray. . . . In 1519 science gains a crushing victory. Magellan makes his famous voyage. . . . Yet even this does not end the war. Many conscientious men oppose the doctrine for two hundred years longer.[128]

White's thesis depicted a warfare "with battles fiercer, with sieges more persistent, with strategy more vigorous than in any of the comparatively petty warfares of Alexander, or Caesar, or Napoleon." The rhetoric "captured the imagination of generations of readers, and his copious references, still impressive, have given his work the appearance of sound scholarship, bedazzling even twentieth-century historians who should know better."[129] Many authors great and small have followed the Draper–White line down to the present. The educated public, seeing so many eminent scientists, philosophers, and scholars in agreement, concluded that they must be right.

In fact, the reason they were in agreement is that they imitated one another. Some historians resisted the warfare idea, and some modern defenders have even gone so far as to argue that science could not have developed without the aiding hand of Christian theology. The reality is that "historical investigation to date has revealed a rich and varied interaction between science and Christianity."[130] Many other historians, however, acquiesced in flattening the medieval earth.[131]

The war continued into the twentieth century in Europe and especially in the United States, where Fundamentalism posed a real threat to the theory of evolution. In Germany, Sigmund Günther on the eve of World War I was still denouncing medieval flat-earth biblical literalism.[132] As late as 1974 J. H. Parry, with no sense of anachronism, transferred both the name and the attitude of American preachers into thirteenth-century philosophers, "the flat-earth fundamentalists."[133] And in 1927 Shipley declared:

More than twenty-five millions of men and women, with ballot in hand, have declared war on modern science. Ostensibly a "war

on the teaching of evolution in our tax-supported schools," the
real issue is much broader and deeper, much more comprehen-
sive in its scope. The deplorable fact must be recognized that in
the United States to-day there exist, side by side, two opposing
cultures, one or the other of which must eventually dominate our
public institutions, political, legal, educational, and social. On
the one side we see arrayed the forces of progress and enlightenment, on the other the forces of reaction, the apostles of tradi-
tionalism. There can be no compromise between these
diametrically opposed armies. If the self-styled Fundamentalists
can gain control over our state and national governments —
which is one of their avowed objectives — much of the best that
has been gained in American culture will be suppressed or
banned, and we shall be headed backwards to the pall of a new
Dark Age.[134]

Long after evolution ceased to be a central issue for society as
a whole, the metaphor of warfare continued, with its implication that Christianity must have opposed the spherical earth.
The Flat Error must be true, it appears, because it fits modern
preconceptions about the Middle Ages. Thus, in 1986, William
O'Neil wrote of the fathers:

Without differentiating amongst the details of their several views
it may be said that they rejected the Hellenistic notion of the
sphericity of the Earth and of the universe in favour of a layered,
flat, square scheme as suggested in Genesis. Indeed to varying
degrees they tended to support the view that the Mosaic Tabernacle represented the shape of the universe. . . . Compromise
. . . went further and further as the medieval centuries passed.[135]

The standard, conventional wisdom lay behind Boorstin's assumptions. He and his audience took the Error for granted.
Boorstin's chapter 13, "The Prison of Christian Dogma," explains that Christians exerted "amnesiac effort to ignore the
growing mass of knowledge [about sphericity] and retreat into

a world of faith and caricature."[136] Chapter 14, "A Flat Earth Returns," paints a picture of sinister ecclesiastical authority enforcing flatness. "To avoid heretical possibilities, faithful Christians preferred to believe there could be no Antipodes, or even, if necessary, that the earth was no sphere. Saint Augustine, too, was explicit and dogmatic." Cosmas occupies two full pages of the book, and "after Cosmas came a legion of Christian geographers each offering his own variant on the Scriptural plan."[137]

By Boorstin's time, the Error had been so firmly established that it was easier to lie back and believe it: easier not to check the sources; easier to fit the consensus; easier to fit the preconceived worldview; easier to avoid the discipline needed in order to dislodge a firmly held error. Religion and science had not been at war until the Draper–White thesis made them so; but the result of the "war" was that "religion" lost, because of

> the process . . . (of which we know next to nothing) by which ideas cease to hold the attention owing to some contagion of discredit or tedium . . . a vague suspicion that science had got the better of it. . . . The logical outcome of the controversy might amount to very little alongside the fatigue of seeing it through to a conclusion.[138]

Boorstin's bibliography indicates that he obtained his ideas not in the sources, but in the works of early twentieth-century historians of geography who rallied to the Draper–White flag.[139] Among these were James Simpson, John Wright, and George Kimble.[140] Simpson, writing in 1925, imposed a flat earth on the fathers, yet admitted that Lactantius is always trotted out as the whipping boy and commented that it is "simply a mistake to consider him in any way as representative of the recognized theological thought and attitude of mind of his day."[141] John Kirtland Wright, who published a thorough book in 1925 on the state of European geography at the time of the crusades, maintained that "on [Isaiah 40] and other scraps even less detailed were erected the medieval arguments in favor of the flatness of the earth." Wright did not identify the scraps. He went on to repeat the error that the sphericity of the earth was "regarded as heretical," by whom and where he does not say. Wright simply desired medieval people to believe in flatness, so while he cited F. S. Betten's article proving that roundness was known throughout the Middle Ages, he buried it by saying that ambivalent texts could be reconciled with a flat-earth doctrine.[142]

Kimble went farther with no more evidence. "Any open confession of interest [in sphericity] would have invited excommunication" in the early Church. It appears that some medievals did believe in sphericity, Kimble grants, but "on the contrary, the relevant passages of their works admit, in some cases, of a construction not incompatible with the flat earth hypothesis." The tortured wording reflects the bias.[143]

Charles Raymond Beazley's history, influential throughout the twentieth century, was the foundation on which these other historians of geography built. In the Middle Ages, Beazley wrote, "everything of value seemed to sink, and only the light and worthless rubbish came floating on down the stream of time." In that period sphericity "gained a hearing" in only a "few cases." He granted that the mappaemundi were theological but then berated them for not being geographical. Among the fathers, "a very strong preponderance of opinion declared itself in favour of substituting for 'sphericism' the obvious truths of a flat earth, vaulted over by the arch of heaven." In the Middle Ages, "the belief in a round or spherical world professed by the Venerable Bede with tolerable clearness, and by some others with varying degrees of confidence, was robbed of all practical value, in the few cases where it gained a hearing."[144] Beazley drew his misapprehensions directly from Antoine-Jean Letronne, who along with Washington Irving, was one of the two nineteenth-century originators of the Flat Error.

One of the earliest portraits of Columbus.

Portrait of Queen Isabella. Ceded and authorized by the Patrimonio Nacional de España.

Columbus before the alleged Council of Salamanca.

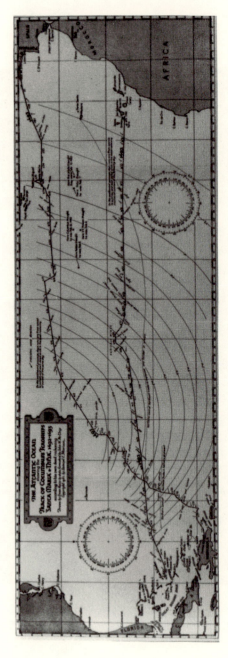

Map of Christopher Columbus's first trip to the New World. From *Admiral of the Ocean Sea: A Life of Christopher Columbus*, by Samuel Eliot Morison. Copyright 1942, © 1970 by Samuel Eliot Morison. By permission of Little, Brown and Company.

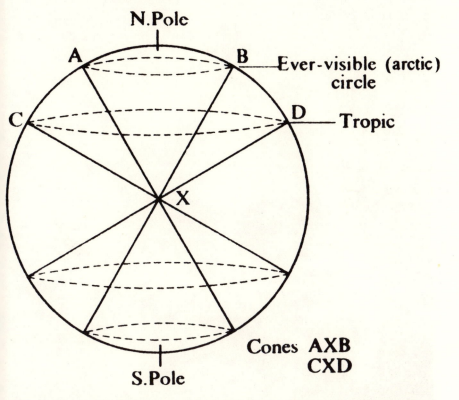

Aristotle's concept of the position and shape of the inhabited world. Reprinted by permission of the publishers and The Loeb Classical Library from *Aristotle: Volume VII, Meteorolgica,* translated by H.D.P. Lee. Cambridge, Mass.: Harvard University Press, 1952.

Bust of Aristotle. By permission of Kunsthistoriches Museum, Vienna.

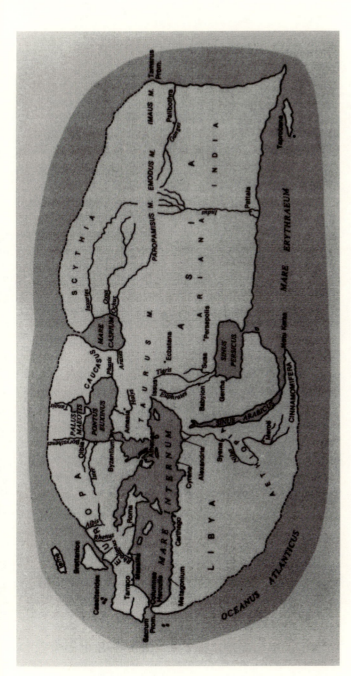

Shape of the inhabited world reconstructed from Strabo. Reprinted by permission of Dover Press from *A History of Ancient Geography Among the Greeks and Romans from the Earliest Ages till the Fall of the Roman Empire*, by Edward Herbert Bunbury. 2 vols., 2nd ed. 1883; republished with new introduction by W. H. Stahl, New York: Dover, 1959.

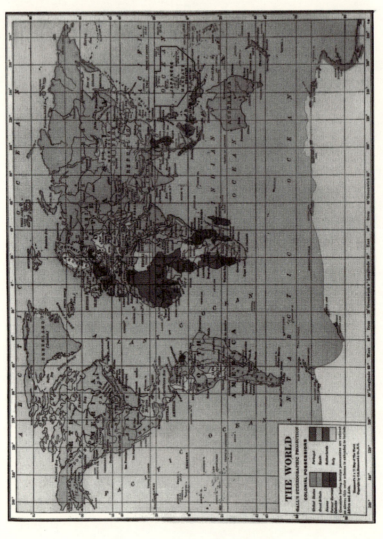

A modern Mercator projection map. A future historian would be unjustified in concluding from this flat map that twentieth-century people believed in a flat earth.

A reconstruction of the world of Claudius Ptolemy. Reprinted by permission of Dover Press from *A History of Ancient Geography Among the Greeks and Romans from the Earliest Ages till the Fall of the Roman Empire*, by Edward Herbert Bunbury. 2 vols., 2nd ed. 1883; republished with new introduction by W. H. Stahl, New York: Dover, 1959.

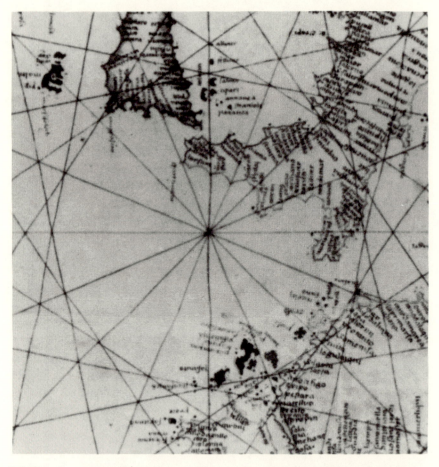

Medieval cartography: Rhumb line centers from a 1449 map by Petrus Roselli. By permission of the Badische Landesbibliothek, Karlsruhe.

The Farnese Atlas: the ancient god holds the spherical world on his shoulders. By permission of Museo Nazionale Archeologico di Napoli.

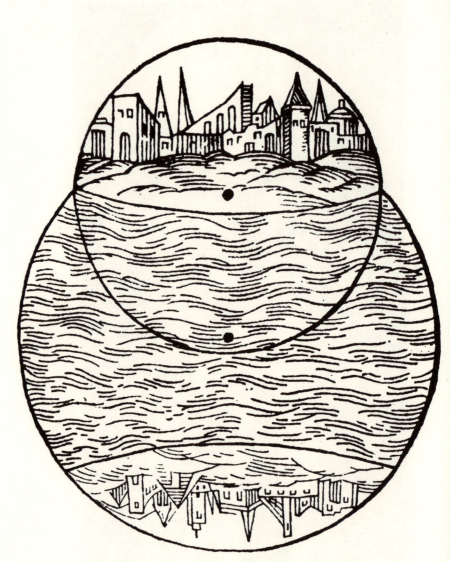

Spheres of earth and water. By permission of W.G.L. Randles.

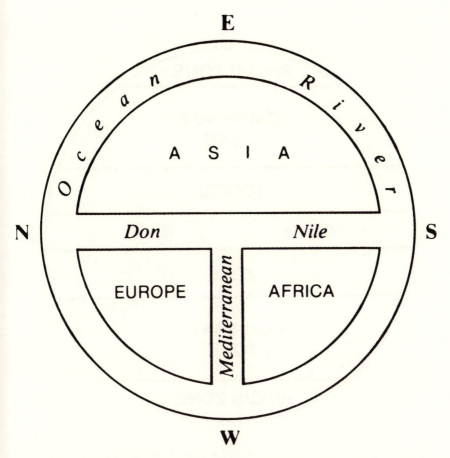

Tri-partite type of medieval mappaemundi. By permission of the publisher and J. B. Harley. From *Cartography in Prehistoric, Ancient, and Medieval Europe and the Mediterranean,* by J. B. Harley and David Woodward, eds. Chicago: University of Chicago Press, 1987.

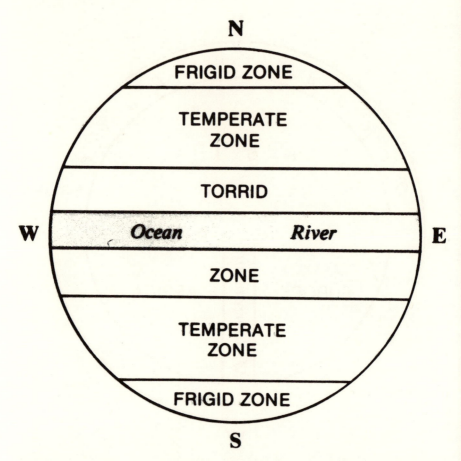

Quadripartite type of mappaemundi. By permission of the publisher and J. B. Harley. From *Cartography in Prehistoric, Ancient, and Medieval Europe and the Mediterranean,* by J. B. Harley and David Woodward, eds. Chicago: University of Chicago Press, 1987.

The ambiguity of the word "round." The *Wizard of Id.* By permission of Johnny Hart and NAS, Inc.

Portrait of Galileo.

Portrait of Copernicus.

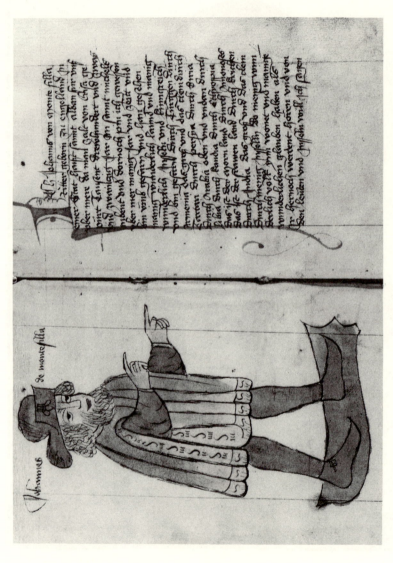

Portrait of John Mandeville. By permission of the Spencer Collection, The New York Public Library; Astor, Lenox and Tilden Foundations.

The earliest known portrait of St. Augustine. By permission of HarperCollins Publishers. From *St. Augustine and His Influence Through the Ages,* by Henri Marrou, translated by Patrick Hepburne-Scott. New York: Harper Torchbooks, 1957. All rights reserved.

Portrait of Petrarch. By permission of Case Western University.

Portrait of Voltaire.

Portrait of Andrew Dickson White. By permission of the Department of Manuscripts and University Archives, Cornell University Library.

Portrait of St. Isidore. By permission of Jacques Fontaine.

Portrait of Washington Irving.

HISTORY

OF THE

LIFE AND VOYAGES

OF

CHRISTOPHER COLUMBUS.

BY WASHINGTON IRVING.

Venient annis
Sæcula seris, quibus Oceanus
Vincula rerum laxet, et ingens
Pateat tellus, Typhisque novos
Detegat Orbes, nec sit terris
Ultima Thule.
Seneca Medea.

A NEW EDITION REVISED AND CORRECTED BY THE AUTHOR.

IN TWO VOLUMES.

VOL. I.

𝔓𝔥𝔦𝔩𝔞𝔡𝔢𝔩𝔭𝔥𝔦𝔞:

CAREY, LEA, & BLANCHARD.

1837.

Title page to Irving's *Life of Columbus.*

A

HISTORY OF NEW-YORK,

FROM THE

BEGINNING OF THE WORLD

TO THE

END OF THE DUTCH DYNASTY.

CONTAINING,

AMONG MANY SURPRISING AND CURIOUS MATTERS,

THE UNUTTERABLE PONDERINGS OF WALTER THE DOUBTER,

THE DISASTROUS PROJECTS OF WILLIAM THE TESTY,

AND

THE CHIVALRIC ACHIEVEMENTS OF PETER THE HEADSTRONG,

THE THREE DUTCH GOVERNORS OF NEW-AMSTERDAM;

BEING THE ONLY

Authentic History of the Times that ever hath been published.

Irving Washington

BY DIEDRICH KNICKERBOCKER.

W. HUGHES SC.

LONDON:

PRINTED FOR THOMAS TEGG, 73, CHEAPSIDE;

RODWELL AND MARTIN, BOND STREET: ALSO, R. GRIFFIN AND CO. GLASGOW.

1824.

R. H.

Title page of Irving's *History of New York*.

CHAPTER FOUR

The Wrong Way Round

The schoolbooks followed the scholars in shifting toward the Flat Error in the late nineteenth century. One reason was the mounting debate over evolution. Another was the prestige of the classics, which produced a number of books extolling the legacy of Greece and Rome, books that contrasted the broad, sunlit uplands of the ancient world with the stinking alleyways of the Middle Ages. Another—in the United States—was a chauvinism that wanted to believe that before the dawn of America broke the world had been in darkness. Columbus's first voyage, for American patriots, was rather like a new day of creation in the freshness of Eden.

Yet another reason was the influence of the most dramatic perpetrator of the Flat Error, Washington Irving (1783–1859), whose romantic tale of Columbus the hero swayed all before him. A textbook by John J. Anderson written in 1880 merely stated that Columbus "believed the earth to be round," but by 1898 Anderson added the scene where Columbus confronts the benighted "wise men" who quote Lactantius at him: "Is there anyone so foolish as to believe that there are people living on the other side of the earth with their heels upward and their heads hanging down?" The wording is not from the sources but is a paraphrase, almost a direct quote, from Irving. Anderson concluded that the wise men believed "that the earth was flat like a plate."[145]

Irving had early conflated history and fiction. He issued his *History of New York from the Beginning of the World to the End of the Dutch Dynasty* (1809) under the pseudonym Diederich Knickerbocker, and he perpetrated a prolonged hoax in order to persuade the reading public that Knickerbocker was a real person.[146] The original idea of the book was to parody pretentious and pedantic historians, but Irving incorporated real historical research, and gradually through subsequent editions he turned the book into a serio-comic epic. "The Author's Apology" to the 1848 edition says that he came to perceive it as a tongue-in-cheek *Aeneid,* since the early days of New York were

> open, like the early and obscure days of ancient Rome, to all the embellishments of heroic fiction. . . . Neither did I conceive I was committing any grievous historical sin in helping out the few facts I could collect . . . with figments of my own brain. . . . My presumptuous trespasses into this . . . region of history have met with deserved rebukes. . . . If it has taken an unwarrantable liberty with our early provincial history, it has at least turned attention to that history and provoked research.[147]

The tone of this apology is ironic. Irving hardly repented — witness his use of Dutch colonial figures as caricatures of modern politicians.

Irving knew how to use libraries and archives, and the public was fooled into taking his literary game as history. Irving mingled fiction with what he announced as a historical reconstruction in his *History of the Life and Voyages of Christopher Columbus* (1828).[148] Irving spent three years in Spain composing Columbus's biography, into which he slipped the dramatic account of Columbus's confrontation with the foolish clergymen at the "council of Salamanca." He set the dramatic stage with the comment that "the Inquisition had just been established in that kingdom, and every opinion that savored of heresy made its owner obnoxious to odium and persecution." Under such dread threat, Columbus appeared at the "convent" in Salamanca as "a simple mariner, standing forth in the midst of an imposing array of professors, friars and dignitaries of the church; maintaining his theory with natural eloquence, and, as it were, pleading the cause of the new world." The University of Salamanca was less at fault, Irving generously allowed, but rather

> the imperfect state of science at the time, and the manner in which knowledge, though rapidly extending, was still impeded in its progress by monastic bigotry. . . . Columbus was assailed with citations from the Bible and the Testament: the book of Genesis, the psalms of David, the orations of the Prophets, the epistles of the apostles, and the gospels of the Evangelists. To these were added expositions of various saints and reverend commentators: St. Chrysostom and St. Augustine, St. Jerome and St. Gregory, St. Basil and St. Ambrose, and Lactantius. . . . A mathematical demonstration was allowed no weight, if it appeared to clash with a text of scripture, or a commentary of one of the fathers. . . . Columbus, who was a devoutly religious man, found that he was in danger of being convicted not merely of error, but of heterodoxy. Others more versed [than the scripture-quoters] in science admitted the globular form of the earth . . . but . . . maintained that it would be impossible to arrive there. . . . Such are specimens of the errors and prejudices, the mingled ignorance and erudition, and the pedantic bigotry, with which Columbus had to contend.[149]

The ironic tension of the account is hard to resist, but it is fabrication, and it is largely upon this fabric that the idea of a medieval flat earth was established.

Samuel Eliot Morison, restrained and judicious as he was, described Irving's version of the meeting at Salamanca as

> pure moonshine. Washington Irving, scenting his opportunity for a picturesque and moving scene, took a fictitious account of this nonexistent university council published 130 years after the

event, elaborated on it, and let his imagination go completely. . . . [This] has become one of the most popular Colum-
bian myths; for we all love to hear of professors and experts being
confounded by simple common sense. . . . The whole story is
misleading and mischievous nonsense. . . . The sphericity of the
globe was not in question. The issue was the width of the ocean;
and therein the opposition was right.[150]

Salvador de Madariaga, the great modern Spanish biographer
of Columbus, referred to the "famous but imaginary confer-
ences at the University of Salamanca and the College of St.
Sebastian."[151]

Besides "letting his imagination go," Irving used his sources
carelessly. He cited Oviedo's *General History of the Indies,* which
has nothing about the council. He cited Ferdinand Columbus's
biography of his father, *The History of the Admiral,* which gives an
extended account of the meeting of the commission in 1486 and
reports no objection to the roundness of the globe. He cited
Remesal, and Remesal made no mention at all of the meeting
at Salamanca. Irving also used Bartolomé de las Casas' *History
of the Indies,* at that time still unpublished, but in Book One,
Chapter Five, Las Casas does refer to the sphericity of the
earth. The modern English translation and paraphrase of las
Casas was itself influenced by Irving, for it suggests that Columbus followed philosophical authority on the roundness of
the earth against unnamed opponents; the original Spanish
gives no hint of such opposition.[152] Madariaga's view is that
Ferdinand Columbus and Bartolomé de las Casas convey a
sense that Talavera was hostile to Christopher Columbus for
political and theological reasons, but in fact, Madariaga observes, Talavera was an able and learned man, and Salamanca,
far from being a hotbed of ignorance, was a center of scientific
knowledge renowned for the exactness of its astronomy and geography and having on its faculty the famous Jewish astronomer Rabbi Abraham Zacuto.[153]

Other than his use of *History of the Indies*, Irving constructed his book from a number of published sources that he found in the Madrid library of Obadiah Rich, a friend who was a book collector. On January 30, 1826, Irving was invited by the U.S. minister in Spain to join the legation, and the minister suggested that he might amuse himself in Madrid by translating Navarrete's collection of documents relating to Columbus's voyages. As Irving had been disappointed at the bad reception accorded his previous work, *Tales of a Traveller* (1824), he thought this a good idea.[154] Having begun, he soon felt confined by Navarrete's compendium, which he considered "dry," and decided to use it as the basis of his own interpretation of the life of Columbus.[155] "Wherever I found a document published by him," he wrote, "I was sure of its correctness, and did not trouble myself to examine the original."[156]

Rich's library, where Irving had a free hand, actually possessed some unedited manuscripts relating to the age of discovery, but Irving set them aside as "minor." What he enjoyed was concocting a dramatic story out of easily available and already known materials. Navarrete might not have been delighted by the enormous commercial and literary success that Irving reaped after less than two years' work on what Navarrete himself had spent a lifetime collecting.

In 1826, when Irving was still in the planning stages of the book, he wrote:

I shall form my narrative from a careful comparison and collation of the works of Las Casas and Columbus' son Ferdinando, both founded on Columbus' Journal — and shall at the same time make use of Oviedo, who lived in Columbus' time and in fact all the old Spanish writers. . . . My brother will be of much assistance to me in my researches and in the examination and collation of facts and dates, about which I mean to be scrupulously attentive and accurate, as I know I shall be expected to be careless in such particulars and to be apt to indulge in the imagination."[157]

Irving completed the whole undertaking, a book of over five hundred pages in its 1981 edition, in twenty-one months. It won both praise and good sales, but Irving "simply did not have the time or the knowledge or the training to make such an investigation. . . . His final claim must rest upon his having turned the story of Columbus into a work of art"[158] in which Christopher plays the hero of a romantic novel, or an epic modern Odysseus or a Faust casting a giant wager against fate, or a mythic American Adam, the First Man of the New World. Irving wanted his history aesthetic, archetypical, and mystical. "The trouble with *Columbus* as history is that there is not enough factual weight to hold it down."[159] Irving said this of the completed *Columbus:* "I have woven into my work many curious particulars not hitherto known concerning Columbus. . . . I have labored hard to make the work complete and accurate. . . I have sought to execute it in such a manner as would render it agreeable to the general reader."[160] Perhaps his "self-deception" was not as "complete" as his biographer Williams thought, for Irving admitted that "to do such a work justice, and execute it as I could execute it, I ought to bestow at least, several more months upon it."[161] Jeffrey Rubin-Dorsky observes that the book

> is not really a 'life' at all, nor does it precisely qualify as 'history.' Although he might have done so had he wanted, since he had access to the very manuscripts Navarrete had spent decades collecting, Irving did not add anything new to the standard, though often contradictory, accounts of the life and voyages that preceded his own. . . . Irving's *Columbus* qualifies, rather, as a work of the imagination . . . he embellishes, heightens, shapes, and colors the events and incidents of his original sources. . . . At times, Irving looks more the fiction writer than the historian.[162]

Irving's *Life of Washington,* written toward the end of his life, shows similar tendencies; it attributed to the first U.S. president a fictitious genealogy and drew upon the patriotic fantasies of Parson Weems.[163] Only a year after *Columbus,* Irving was already playing Knickerbocker again. In 1829 he published *A Chronicle of the Conquest of Granada,* allegedly taken from the manuscripts of "Fray Antonio Agapida," just as *New York* had allegedly been taken from the manuscripts of "Diederich Knickerbocker;" the friar was as fictitious as the Dutchman. Irving himself wrote of "Fray Antonio" that "this was a nom de guerre to enable me to assume greater freedom and latitude in the execution of the work, and to mingle a tinge of romance and satire with the grave historical details."[164] The "chronicle" was a satire of King Ferdinand of Spain in Irving's time by using the character of King Ferdinand of Spain in Columbus's, but in the revised edition of the book Irving maintained that the work was "true history." In 1829, Irving published a semifictional account of *The Voyages and Discoveries of the Companions of Columbus.* In the preface he wrote that the "extraordinary actions and adventures of these men, while they rival the exploits recorded in chivalric romance, have the additional interest of verity."[165] Irving introduced in his influential biography of Columbus a Flat Error that was historically unnecessary. Irving was good at fiction. His contemporary, less dramatic a writer but a better historian, William Prescott (1796–1859) presented an entire *History of Ferdinand and Isabella* without once bringing up the idea of flatness.[166] Irving's tale of the "Council of Salamanca" must be placed in its chronological context: the anticatholicism and anti-Spanish bias of Irving's native country, and the growth in the early nineteenth-century of strange hollow-earth and flat-earth theories by New England sectarians, may have linked with Irving's observation of the backwardness of the church in Spain in his own day to create in his mind the sense that his tale of the dreadful council was somehow "morally right," regardless of the historical facts. And Irving, who was well-traveled in Europe (he spent seventeen years abroad) and had wide historical and geographical interests, might also have heard of the Flat-Earth Errors emerging in the French academy at the same time.[167]

The late nineteenth-century Errors drew their color from

Irving's account, but their scientific and historical point of view was that of the French Institute and Academy instead.

The old Académie Royale des Sciences was closed down by the Revolution in 1793. In 1795, an Institut National was founded under the Constitution of the Year Three of the Republic to replace the old academies. The Institut broke completely with its royal and clerical antecedents; supported by Talleyrand, Mirabeau, and Condorcet, its ideological basis was that of the Encyclopedists of the Enlightenment. It was divided into three "classes," one of which was for the sciences. After the restoration of the monarchy, this section was reconstituted in 1816 as the new Académie des sciences.[168] From 1795 onward, even after the restoration, the Institute/Academy propagated Enlightenment progressivism, becoming the seedbed of middle-class belief in the skeptical teachings of Voltaire.

The man who established the Flat Error as an academic commonplace was Antoine-Jean Letronne (1787–1848). Letronne seems to have confected it as a result of his studies with Edmé Mentelle (1730–1815), who taught him geography, and Jean-Baptiste Gail (1755–1829), who gave him access to the writings of the church fathers by teaching him Greek.

Under the Institut's class of sciences, the Section of Geography was led by Mentelle. Even before the Revolution, interest in geography had been growing, with much public attention fixed on travels both true and fictional, upon exotic lands (Turkey and Japan were particularly popular), and upon the first organized scientific expeditions. Geography was a "hot subject" right through the late eighteenth and early nineteenth century, and Mentelle and his colleagues enjoyed a wide audience.

Mentelle was well known in his own time as a popular Voltairean historian who wrote treatises promoting the Enlightenment for young readers; he attracted the most attention for his depiction of Jesus Christ as an impostor.[169] Under the 1803 reorganization of the Institut, Mentelle dominated the *classe* or section that corresponded to the old Académie des inscriptions. Known for his manipulation of both politics and science, Mentelle was in turn an enthusiastic supporter of the Republic, of Napoleon, and of Louis XVIII, from whom he received the Cross of the Legion of Honour. Given the shifting grounds of external, national politics, a political academic could undermine his academic rivals by labeling them as royalists or, later in turn, as Bonapartists.

Gail, like Mentelle, courted every government, receiving honors from both Louis XVIII and Czar Alexander I. A polemicist, he wrote a vast number of pamphlets and open letters attacking his academic adversaries. He eventually came to believe that there was a cabal of scholars against him, and at one point he even took a former student to court.

Mentelle perceived the Middle Ages as a period of ignorance, a time of "profound night" lasting twelve centuries. Still, the distinguished and influential astronomer Jean-Baptiste Delambre, Mentelle's contemporary, argued correctly that there is no way of determining the modern equivalents of the measurements of the globe made by ancient or medieval geographers and every reason to doubt that without modern instruments they could have been very accurate, but he assumed that their efforts to calculate degrees were necessarily based on the assumption of sphericity. Mentelle and Delambre left the Flat Error to Mentelle's pupil Letronne, who explicitly argued that the fathers and their medieval successors had affirmed a flat earth.[170]

Letronne's influence among scholars was deeper than Washington Irving's. Letronne's eulogists deemed him a secular saint: he supported his widowed mother and his younger brother, who never returned him sufficient gratitude; he married a wealthy woman with whom he had ten children and did secret acts of charity that remained unknown until after his death. He was a brilliant wit and formidable antagonist, yet always took pains to avoid hurting feelings.

Mentelle, struck by the young Letronne's intelligence, made him his collaborator in a number of works, including the four-volume *Histoire de géographie moderne* (Paris, 1806). Letronne

studied Latin, Greek, Mathematics, and Egyptology. He ac-
quired a wealthy patron with whom he traveled throughout
French-occupied Europe under the Empire. Like his mentors,
he got on well with all governments, from Napoleon through
Louis XVIII and Charles X to the monarchy of Louis-
Philippe, and after his death he was eulogized under the reign
of Louis-Napoleon. In 1817 he became director of the Ecole des
Chartes and in 1819 Inspector General of the University of
Paris. As with Mentelle, his interests extended to history as well
as geography, and in 1831 he obtained the chair of history at
the Collège de France. He was a keen polemicist, writing a critical history of Christianity in 1833 and in 1844 a treatise dis-
proving the authenticity of a supposed relic of Saint Louis.[171]

Letronne's prestige was so great that Charles Raymond
Beazley and the others accepted his views without checking his
sources. His article "On the Cosmographical Opinions of the
Church Fathers" (1834) became the basis of Beazley's and later
historians' treatment of the fathers. The article's attitude appears from the first sentence, which announced that until recently it was believed that all science had to be based on the
Bible. Obliged to admit that the two most seminal Christian
thinkers, Augustine and Origen, taught quite the opposite, Letronne evaded the corollary by assigning them to a minority
and by claiming that the majority insisted on a "literal" interpretation. Later he accused Augustine, Basil, and Ambrose of
holding the same errors as Lactantius and Severian.

Under such an alleged reign of folly, Letronne wrote, astronomers were "forced" to believe that the earth was a flat surface,
suspended miraculously in space. A few theologians did know
the earth was round; the majority, however, were flat-earthers
who, despite the stupidity of their views, "had three irresistible
arguments; persecution, prison, and the stake."[172] He admitted
that Photius rejected Cosmas Indicopleustes but proceeded
nevertheless with a six-page detailed exposition of Cosmas's
follies, implying that Cosmas's theories were significant and influential. This undue attention to Cosmas influenced Beazley
to make the same mistake.

The flat-earth theories, Letronne continued, dominated up to the time of Columbus and Magellan and even persisted afterward, but finally the discoveries of Kepler, Huygens, and Newton erased the childish ideas that the theologians had defended inch by inch as orthodox. A brilliant and incisive scholar, Letronne immediately had many imitators, for example the Vicomte de Santarem, who drew upon Irving as well.[173]

Letronne was, with Irving, the founding father of the Flat Error, for flatness had not attracted much attention from the great philosophes of the eighteenth-century Enlightenment. The great satirist Voltaire (1694–1778) only distantly alluded to it in the article "The Sky of the Ancients" in his *Dictionary* by saying that the ancient Hebrews had believed the earth and sky to be flat. The implication that the Christians believed the same is left hanging. In his famous *Essay on Customs,* he described Columbus's struggle against the "prejudices" of his contemporaries but suggested neither here nor in his treatment of Magellan that these contemporaries thought the earth was flat.[174] The eighteenth-century writers Condillac (1714–1780), Condorcet (1743–1794), Diderot (1713–1784), Benjamin Franklin (1706–1790), Gibbon (1737–1794), Hume (1711–1776), and Robertson (1721–1793), were unstinting in their contempt for Christianity and for the Middle Ages in particular. Condorcet, for example, said that disregard for human sciences (as opposed to theology) is a prime characteristic of Christianity; he dismissed the Middle Ages as a time of "theological dreaming," "superstitious impostures," and "ignorant stupidity." Nonetheless, the philosophes had little to say about flatness.[175] Gibbon wrote, with uncharacteristic muddle, that "the orthodox faith confined the habitable world to *one* temperate zone, and represented the earth as an oblong surface." Gibbon derided Cosmas but ironically fell into the same error as Columbus himself by confusing an oblong representation of the known world with an oblong conception of the entire earth. The unbridled Tom Paine (1737–1809) wrote that "Vigilius [Vergil of Salzburg] was condemned to be burned [!] for asserting the antipodes, or in other words, that the earth was a globe. . . . There was no moral ill in believing that the earth was flat like a trencher, any more than there was moral virtue in believing it was round like a globe. . . . But when a system of religion is made to grow out of a supposed system of creation that is not true, . . . the result is foolish."[176]

The Error was seldom in evidence earlier. The rationalist precursors of the Enlightenment never mentioned it, though it underlay an occasional comment. Thomas Hobbes's *Leviathan* (1651) boasted that "our own Navigations make manifest, and all men learned in humane Sciences, now acknowledge there are Antipodes," but in darker ages those who "but supposed such Doctrine . . . have been punished for it by Authority Ecclesiasticall. . . . We may justly pronounce for the Authors of all this Spirituall Darknesse, the Pope, and Roman Clergy."[177] John Wilkins was a rare exception to the rule, writing in 1708 explicitly about the flat earth. He suggested that humans eventually might be able to travel to the moon and inhabit it, and compared himself and his detractors to Columbus and the alleged flat-earthers. Wilkins offered an eccentrically long list of alleged flat-earthers, including Herodotus and Lucretius along with Chrysostom, Augustine, Procopius, and of course Lactantius.[178]

Protestant opponents of Roman Catholicism avoided the Error. The Reformers all believed in a spherical earth, because all were in touch with traditional philosophical learning, where that view was universally held. They wished to uphold the authority of the Bible in religion against the authority of philosophy, contemporary philosopher-scientists, as well as medieval philosopher-scholastics, but they accepted natural science as valid in its own subject.[179]

Nor is there more than a hint of the Error in the sixteenth and early seventeenth centuries among the revolutionary cosmologists such as Copernicus, Galileo, and Campanella. Galileo (1564–1642), famous for provoking censure for his claim that science could not only describe observations but actually discern the truth independent of revelation, had a particular and sophisticated reason for being cautious. He wished to reconcile his teaching with the fathers, and so avoid unnecessary conflict. Precisely because the Bible does not clearly describe the structure of the cosmos, and precisely because the fathers — he cited St. Augustine — maintained that where revelation is silent we may follow philosophy, Galileo argued that it was legitimate for astronomy to proceed without reference to revelation. He was combating the remnants of the old Aristotelian system, one of whose hallmarks was spheres, including of course the sphericity of the earth, so he wasted no words arguing against a flat-earth doctrine that he knew no one favored anyhow.[180]

Thomas Campanella's *Defense of Galileo* was composed while the author, a Dominican friar, was in prison in 1616 for his defense of Copernican astronomy. Hostile to the papal bureaucracy that had victimized him and intent on defending heliocentricity against its clerical detractors, Campanella had every reason to blacken his persecutors by comparing their stupidity to those of the flat-earthers. But other than a reference in chapter three to the fathers' denial of the existence of antipodeans and a sharper cut in the same chapter against theologians being influenced by "heathen philosophy" to believe in such nonsense as night being produced by the sun's going behind a large mountain in the north, Campanella did not suggest that anyone believed in a flat earth.[181] Johannes Kepler's "Defense of Tycho" (1600), sharply defended Tycho Brahe against obscurantists, but he included nothing about a flat earth.[182]

Other great skeptics of the sixteenth century, such as Michel de Montaigne (1533–1592), François Rabelais (1495–1553), Giordano Bruno (c. 1548–1600), and even Francis Bacon (1561–1626), the great crusader against Christian superstition, showed little interest in flatness. Bacon's only reference is vague: "How great opposition and prejudice natural philosophy had received by superstition, and the immoderate and blind zeal of religion . . . the cosmographers which first discovered and described the roundness of the earth, and the consequence thereof touching the *Antipodes,* were not much otherwise censured by the ancient fathers of the Christian Church."[183]

The seed that Letronne and his followers would cultivate was planted by Nicholas Copernicus (1473–1543) in his classical work demonstrating the solar system, *De revolutionibus, On the Revolutions.*[184] In the preface, Copernicus used Lactantius to illustrate how the ignorance of opponents of the round earth was comparable to that of those insisting on geocentricity in his own time.

> Perhaps there will be babblers who claim to be judges of astronomy although completely ignorant of the subject and, badly distorting some passage of Scripture to their purpose, will dare to find fault with my undertaking and censure it. I disregard them even to the extent of despising their criticism as unfounded. For it is not unknown that Lactantius, otherwise an illustrious writer but hardly an astronomer, speaks quite childishly about the earth's shape, when he mocks those who declared that the earth has the form of a globe. Hence scholars need not be surprised if any such persons will likewise ridicule me. Astronomy is written for astronomers.[185]

This passage is remarkable in a number of ways.

First, what Copernicus did *not* say is remarkable. He did not say that Lactantius was typical of either the church fathers or of medieval thinking, or even that anyone at all shared his views. On the contrary, when later in book one, chapter three, he attacked other flat-earthers he found them in the ancient pagan world rather than in the medieval world. Further, as a canon of the Catholic Church, Copernicus did not claim that theologians promoted the flat earth and in fact took care not even to identify Lactantius as a church father. Copernicus's preface, addressed to Pope Paul III, was couched in the standard rhetoric used at the time to obtain ecclesiastical patronage. Perhaps Copernicus felt secure in attacking Lactantius because of Lactantius's longstanding taint of heresy.

Second, the passage was the basis for later writers using Lactantius as a villain illustrating a medieval belief in a flat earth. Despite Copernicus's caution and his own Catholic faith, the papacy later found the passage about Lactantius offensive and in 1616 ordered it stricken from further editions of the book. But this was too late to affect the third edition of 1617, and since no further edition appeared until 1854, the three editions that were influential for three centuries were all unexpurgated.

The Renaissance Humanists did not merely attack the Middle Ages; they invented them.[186] The Humanists perceived themselves as restoring ancient letters, arts, and philosophy. The more they presented themselves as heroic restorers of a glorious past, the more they had to argue that what had preceded them was a time of darkness. "For this golden century, as it were, has brought back to light the liberal arts, which were all but extinguished: grammar, poetry, oratory, painting, sculpture, architecture, music."[187] There was also a political motive: the Italian humanists wanted to promote the independence of the Italian cities by denying the legitimacy of the Holy Roman Empire. For them, there was no "transfer of empire" (*translatio imperii*) from Rome to the Germanic emperors that followed Charlemagne and Otto the Great.

Where Protestants wished to darken the Middle Ages in order to discredit the papacy, Humanists such as Erasmus wished to restore the purity of the early church, which coincided with the late classical age of the early Roman Empire. Both the Protestants and the Humanists, demanding the restoration of a brilliant past, needed to posit a decline. The fifth century was a perfect date for them to begin this decline: in 476 the last Roman emperor in the West was deposed, and the Italians could argue that this was the end of legitimate imperial authority; the Protestants could point to Augustine (d. 430) as the last legitimate church father and the Council of Chalcedon (451) as the last legitimate ecumenical council. After that: darkness.

The brighter the Humanists were to shine, the darker the preceding ages had to be painted. Petrarch (1304–1374), the first Humanist, invented the term "Dark Ages" about 1340. Petrarch divided history into "ancient" (*antiqua*), before the adoption of Christianity by the Roman Empire (fourth century), and "modern" (*nova*).[188] From Petrarch's time onward, Humanist historians concentrated on writing either about the ancient world or about recent or contemporary history.[189] This left a growing sense that between the Good Classics and the Good Renaissance was a dark period of illegitimate authority in church and state and ignorance of arts and philosophy, a dark age when (as in the late twentieth century) Greek, Latin, the classics, and the Bible were little known.

But, as Walter Berschin recently observed:

> It has long been known that there was no direct "line of connection between the Renaissance and antiquity," that "not a single Roman writer was newly discovered," that the script which was revived at that time, on models presumed to be ancient, was the Carolingian (in its Italian form of the high Middle Ages), and that the manuscripts of ancient works, freed from the "gloomy dungeons" of the monasteries into the glorious freedom of humanistic private ownership [and many of these were lost by theft or carelessness] . . . had their origin almost without exception in medieval . . . scriptoria.[190]

The Humanists did not mention flatness, but as the idea grew that the people in the intervening ages were stupid, so did the assumption that nothing was too silly for them to believe.

The term "Middle Ages" originated in the fifteenth century and was popularized in the seventeenth century by Christoph Keller's *Historia medii aevi* (1675), which had eight editions by 1732.[191] The "Middle Ages" were invented just as a common method of periodizing history was emerging. Before about 1650 there was no generally accepted method: many different systems jostled one another. Local dating was the most common; systems of universal dating included the use of papal or imperial reigns, the "four kingdoms" from the Book of Daniel, the "seven ages," and the Anno Domini (the year from the birth of Christ). By the sixteenth century there were abortive efforts to date from the year of creation (little agreement could be

found there).[192] Thus the "Dark Ages" invented by the Humanists was easily connected with the "Middle Ages" invented by
the periodizers, and the connection was fixed by such powerful
works as Gibbon's *Decline and Fall of the Roman Empire* (1781),
which portrayed the Middle Ages as the triumph of Christianity and barbarism. Henry St. John Bolingbroke (1678–1751),
sharing Gibbon's contempt, wrote that to study the Middle
Ages is "a ridiculous affectation in any man who means to be
useful to the present age."[193]

This dichotomy, this break between ages, is a peculiar form
of Platonic reification of a merely convenient periodization.
Such a break between the "ancients" and the "moderns" is historically impossible, for historical thought always requires an
understanding of continuing development through time, a
process of getting from A to C by way of B.[194] But the idea of the
dark Middle Ages is still fixed in the popular consciousness. No
caricature is too preposterous to be accepted. Here is a popular
children's book of the early twentieth century:

> Between the far away past history of the world, and that which
> lies near to us; in the time when the wisdom of the ancient times
> was dead and had passed away, and our own days of light had not
> yet come, there lay a great black gulf in human history, a gulf of
> ignorance, of superstition, of cruelty, and of wickedness.
>
> That time we call the dark or middle ages. Few records remain
> to us of that dreadful period of our world's history, and we only
> know of it through broken and disjointed fragments that have
> been handed down to us through the generations.[195]

We have seen how the Error was established. The question
now is why it persists.

Around the Corner

This concluding chapter offers a chronological summary of geographical knowledge and a discussion of the evolution in the twentieth century of accurate historical views on medieval sphericity, and ends with suggestions as to why the Flat Error continues to persist.

From the fourth century B.C. almost all the Greek philosophers maintained the sphericity of the earth; the Romans adopted the Greek spherical views; and the Christian fathers and early medieval writers, with few exceptions, agreed. During the Middle Ages, Christian theology showed little if any tendency to dispute sphericity. In the early Middle Ages, interest in natural science was limited, although geography and astronomy formed part of the liberal arts curriculum that dominated early medieval education and remained the core of the university curriculum throughout the Middle Ages. The shape of the earth was not widely discussed, since interests tended to be focused on theological issues. Among the uneducated a variety of vague ideas seem to have been common, but among the educated always existed a consensus that the earth was spherical. With the reintroduction of Aristotelian science in the twelfth century and of Ptolemaic geography in the fifteenth, medieval ideas of the sphericity of the globe became sharper and more exact than ever before. Further, when the

increasingly commercial economy of the fifteenth century
prompted navigational explorations of new markets, the mind-
set shifted to embrace the practical knowledge of geography for
the sake of exploiting the new markets as well as for the older
goal of making more converts to Christianity.

Educated medieval opinion was virtually unanimous that the
earth was round, and there is no way whatever that Columbus's
voyages even claimed to demonstrate the fact. The idea that
"Columbus showed that the world was round" is an invention.
The soil was prepared for the invention by the Humanists and
Protestants; its seed was the Copernican controversy. Scrupulously adhering to the facts himself, Copernicus attacked the
conservative defenders of the geocentric universe by comparing
them with Lactantius, the one church father who clearly rejected sphericity. Copernicus was careful not to blanket either
ancient or medieval Christians with Lactantius's error. Even in
the seventeenth century scientific writers such as Galileo and
Campanella made no point of the Flat Error, although it is possible that some of the Error's popularity later came from a confusion in the popular mind between the case of Galileo, who
was prosecuted, and Copernicus, who was not.

In the seventeenth century, with the growth of what Amos
Funkenstein calls "secular theology," a new worldview began to
emerge.[196] In the first stages, coherence was maintained: theology, philosophy, and science were seen to be part of one united
search for truth but now with empirical and especially mathematical models replacing the old scholastic ones. In the seventeenth century, and even through most of the eighteenth,
educated people still commonly lived a double intellectual life,
tending to receive both Christian tradition and natural science
without facing the epistemological contradictions. On the one
hand, truth came from revelation transmitted by tradition and
scripture; on the other hand it came from mathematics and ex-
periment. Logically, one could choose one or the other, or one
could attempt the difficult task of reconciling them. Most
eighteenth-century writers chose the fourth option: evading the
question. After the insecurity bred by the religious wars and

social upheavals of the sixteenth and seventeenth centuries there was a generally felt need to avoid conflict and also to impose order or "laws" on a nature so as to control it.

In the next phase, from early in the eighteenth century, philosophical rationalism culminating in the work of Immanuel Kant gradually limited the place of theology and replaced it in many areas, such as ethics, where it had previously held sway. During the century, the idea of natural science narrowed and focused on problems that could be investigated by mathematics and tested by physical evidence. By the end of the eighteenth century, the methods of theology, philosophy, and natural science had diverged. Still it was accepted by most intellectual leaders that an accommodation between science and theology was both feasible and desirable. Most surprisingly, the vehement anticlericals of the Enlightenment seldom made the Flat Error. They were concerned with attacking the scholastics and their successors for being hidebound Aristotelians, and they were fully aware that sphericity was central to Aristotle's cosmology.

During the nineteenth century it became increasingly common to opt for scientific realism or positivism and to tolerate theology only insofar as it abandoned its proper epistemology in favor of a scientific basis. In the later nineteenth century, many philosophers and scientists were vigorously attacking the position that theology had an epistemological basis of its own, and by the end of the century they had been so successful in establishing their viewpoint that they were outraged — or dumfounded — that relics of it persisted. Christian epistemology was identified with an outmoded, obsolete, medieval worldview, and because that worldview is so foreign to the modern, progressivist worldview, it was misunderstood as superstition. Thus it came to seem natural, obvious, certain, that medieval people were so superstitious that they *must have* believed in something as foolish as the flat earth. The few actual medieval flat-earthers were belabored to confirm the prejudice, and the bulk of the evidence on the other side was ignored.

Once the controversy over evolution faded, philosophers and

historians of science were able to take a longer view of the relationship between Christianity and science, and in so doing, to
dispel the Flat Error.[197] It was just when the Error was being
firmly established in the early twentieth century that the first
concerted efforts were made to dispel it. At first the efforts
came largely either from Catholic writers wishing to preserve
their religion from the imputation of having defended a flat
earth, or from professional medievalists with a stake in rescuing
their chosen period from the pejorative label "Dark Ages."

At the turn of the century, Pierre Duhem (1861–1916) made
an apologistic but learned defense of medieval thought. He was
a physicist and considered himself a positivist; he was also a
Catholic. His wish to resolve the tension between the two as-
pects of his thought led him to a thorough study of the sources,
ending in his monumental *Système du monde*. There he showed
that medieval thinkers made no distinction between theology
and science.[198] He also argued that on the whole the medieval
church had supported and promoted natural philosophy and
was the precursor and founder of modern science. Duhem's
work overcorrected for the progressivists and has since required
correction by more recent historians of science, who restrict or
downplay the importance of scholastic theology in the origins of
modern natural science.[199] In the 1920s, the growth of medieval
studies in both Europe and the United States reached the point
where Charles Homer Haskins (d. 1929) at Harvard argued
that a Renaissance had already occurred in the twelfth century.[200] Lynn Thorndike (1882–1965) of Columbia argued in
his *History of Magic and Experimental Science* that medieval theology promoted science. Thorndike observed that Lactantius was
not typical of patristic or medieval thought and that Beazley
had cited Letronne without checking the sources.[201] This clear
warning in Thorndike's monumental work did not deter later
historians of geography from imitating Beazley's imitation of
Letronne.

In the 1920s, Alfred North Whitehead (1861–1947) argued
that the immediate precursor to modern science was more to be

found in the scholastic emphasis on reason, organization, and encyclopedic knowledge than in the discursive, speculative thought of the Greeks. He agreed with Thorndike that the scholastic realists, who believed that God was utter rationality and that the rationality of the human mind was in the image and likeness of God, made the development of science possible. Later, Alexandre Koyré (1892–1964) took a corrective view to the Duhem-Whitehead position, claiming that modern science is in discontinuity with that of Greece, the Middle Ages, and even the nineteenth century, for modern scientists are less concerned with "truth" than with determining which hypotheses work best with the evidence. Modern philosophy of science tends to retreat from scientific realism toward the view that every statement is a statement about human concepts, which may have nothing to do with an external "reality" that is always unknowable.[202]

Some revisionists began to address the Error head on. F. S. Betten, a Jesuit, defined his task with unnecessary caution, arguing only that in each century of Christianity there had been at least one writer affirming sphericity.[203] Charles W. Jones, a distinguished professor of English at Cornell and then at Berkeley, confronted the Error more broadly, demonstrating its falsehood by citing a range of medieval philosophers and poets. Writing in 1934, Jones was already astonished that the Error still persisted in defiance of well-established evidence.[204]

In the same year Michael Foster (d. 1959), tutor in philosophy at Oxford, followed Whitehead in arguing that the medieval theological view of a cosmos planned by a single rational Deity was essential for the development of science.[205] George Sarton (1884–1956), a chemist who established the history of science as a discipline at Harvard, saw that the question of sphericity in the Middle Ages did not lie between flat-earthers and round-earthers but between round-earthers and those who found the question uninteresting. He distinguished properly between sphericity and the antipodes: "The Church never had a serious hostility to the idea of sphericity, but it could not brook the suggestion of a polygenetic humanity; its objections were not geographical but anthropological."[206]

By 1943 the Flat Error prompted the Historical Association of Britain to publish a pamphlet. The author, Eva Taylor, offered a balanced view, citing Lactantius and Cosmas but pointing out that "all the more scholarly of the fathers" accepted sphericity, as did the medieval philosophers. She noted that Sacrobosco's treatise on the sphere had thirty editions between 1478 and 1501 and concluded that "it is difficult to understand why the story has gained such ground that prior to Columbus's voyage it was generally believed that the world was flat."[207]

Contemporary and recent historians of science corrected Draper and White by seeing that the relationship between science and the intellectual establishment in Christian Europe could not be characterized simply. There was no one "patristic view" or "early medieval view" or "scholastic view," but a diversity of views. Lactantius's ideas were atypical, and the church fathers who tried to make the Bible a textbook for natural science were in the minority. As the medieval philosophers gathered classical and contemporary thought together into coherent systems, they became aware of the gaps and the weak spots in existing knowledge and attempted to fill and mend them with new research. Thus the impressive theoretical and experimental works of Robert Grosseteste, Roger Bacon, Nicole Oresme, and Jean Buridan. "The great new scientific theories of the sixteenth and seventeenth centuries all originate from rents torn by scholastic criticism in the fabric of Aristotelian thought. Most of those theories also embody key concepts created by scholastic science."[208]

With historians and philosophers undercutting the reductionist assumption that science was the only way to truth, the road was cleared for a new generation of historians of science to operate on a sophisticated level.[209] Edward Grant, David Lindberg, David Woodward, Robert S. Westman, and others are recasting the scenario in more balanced and accurate terms. Woodward writes:

The medieval period consists of several entirely different sub-periods and it is unwise to assume that the views of a few individuals can be extended to the period as a whole. . . . Nineteenth-century writers also oversimplified and underestimated medieval thinkers' understanding of the physical world; this is reflected in the frequently repeated views that most medieval scholars thought the earth was flat. . . . Undue space in general historical texts [was] given to Cosmas Indicopleustes.[210]

Despite the work of modern historians of science, the Error continues to be almost as persistent as in the educated mind as it was nearly a century ago. "Flat-earthers" is shorthand for ignoramuses. "All reasonable people accept the results of repeatable scientific experiments. If they don't, they are rightly regarded (or disregarded) as flat-Earthers."[211] Why, especially after famous, respected, and widely read authors such as Morison and Madariaga contemptuously dismissed it half a century ago, does the error persist? What can the Flat Error teach us about human knowledge and our own worldview? First, historians, scientists, scholars, and other writers often wittingly or unwittingly repeat and propagate errors of fact or interpretation. No one can be automatically believed or trusted without checking methodology and sources. Second, scholars and scientists often are led by their biases more than by the evidence. Third, historians, who could be expected by the nature of their trade to understand that every worldview is a human construct and that paradigms of knowledge are precarious and inevitably change, including the religious, scientific realist, and positivist worldviews, sometimes forgot that there are and can be no privileged systems by which to judge the truth of other systems. Skepticism can be applied not only to reputed facts but also to accepted theories, models, intellectual fads, views of the world. Whether God creates meaning, the cosmos creates meaning, or humanity creates meaning, meaning is both arbitrary and absolute. There is no higher meaning by which meaning can be judged.

Fourth, the modern view combining relativism and progress as widely understood is incoherent. A true relativism would assume that no worldview is better than another; a true progressivism would assume that worldviews are moving closer and closer to a predetermined and preferred goal.[212] The two beliefs are mutually exclusive. The assumption of the superiority of "our" views to that of older cultures is the most stubborn remaining variety of ethnocentrism. If we were not so ethnocentrically convinced of the ignorance or stupidity of the Middle Ages, we would not fall into the Flat Error. And we would not remain in it if we were not afraid of the conceptual shock of realizing that our closest held assumptions are precarious. The hope that we are making progress toward a goal (which is not defined and about which there is no consensus) leads us to undervalue the past in order to convince ourselves of the superiority of the present.[213]

Finally, fallacies or "myths" of this nature take on a life of their own, creating a dialectic with each other and eventually making a "cycle of myths" reinforcing one another. For example, it has been shown that "The Inquisition" never existed, but that fallacy, like the flat earth fallacy, is part of the "cycle" that includes the Dark Ages, the Black Legend, the opposition of Christianity to science, and so on. The cycle becomes so embedded in our thought that it helps to form our worldview in ways that make it impervious to evidence. We are so convinced that medieval people *must* have been ignorant enough to think the world flat that when the evidence is thrown in front of us we avoid it, as we might, when driving, swerve around an obstacle in the road. Thus our worldview is based more upon what we think happened than what really happened. A shared body of "myth" can overwhelm reason and evidence, as it did in Nazi Germany. Caution is called for, to put it mildly.

But the search for truth is long and laborious and easily set aside. And since the present is transformed day by day, minute by minute, second by second, into the past, while the future is unknown and unknowable, we are left on the dark sea without stars, without compass or astrolabe, more unsure of our position and our goal than any of Columbus's sailors. The terror of meaninglessness, of falling off the edge of knowledge, is greater than the imagined fear of falling off the edge of the earth. And so we prefer to believe a familiar error than to search, unceasingly, the darkness.

Notes

1. Marcia Bartusiak, "Mapping the Universe," *Discover* (August 1990): 63.

2. Personal communication to the author, 1990.

3. C. S. Lewis, *The Discarded Image* (Cambridge, 1964), 140–41.

4. Cecil Jane, ed., *Select Documents Illustrating the Four Voyages of Columbus,* 2 vols. (London, 1930–1933), 1:xxii.

5. Among the twentieth-century works attempting to dispel the error are F. S. Betten, "Knowledge of the Sphericity of the Earth During the Earlier Middle Ages," *Catholic Historical Review* 3 (1923): 74–90; Anna-Dorothee von den Brincken, "Die Kugelgestalt der Erde in der Kartographie des Mittelalters," *Archiv für Kulturgeschichte* 58 (1976): 77–95; Pierre Duhem, *Le système du monde: Histoire des doctrines cosmologiques de Platon à Copernic,* 10 vols. (Paris, 1913–1959); Edward Grant, *Physical Science in the Middle Ages* (New York, 1971); J. B. Harley and David Woodward, *The History of Cartography,* vol. 1, *Cartography in Prehistoric, Ancient, and Medieval Europe and the Mediterranean* (Chicago, 1987); Charles W. Jones, "The Flat Earth," *Thought* 9 (1934): 296–307; David C. Lindberg and Ronald L. Numbers, eds., *God and Nature* (Berkeley, Calif., 1986); David C. Lindberg, *Science in the Middle Ages* (Chicago, 1978); David C. Lindberg and Ronald L. Numbers, "Beyond War and Peace: A Reappraisal of the Encounter between Christianity and Science," *Church History* 55 (1986): 338–54; W.G.L. Randles, *De la terre plate au globe terrestre: Une mutation épistémologique rapide (1480–1520)* [Cahiers des annales 38] (Paris, 1980).

6. For example, since 1900: An Anonymous *Introductory History of the United States* (Sacramento, Calif., 1900), 2; Calista McCabe Courtenay, *Christopher Columbus* (New York, 1917), 6; José Forgione, *Historia general,* 10th ed., Buenos Aires, 1920), 168; J. Lynn Barnard and A. O. Roorbach, *Epochs of World Progress* (New York, 1927), 352–53; A. Gokovsky and O. Trachtenberg, *History of Feudalism* (Moscow, 1934), 127; Carlos Cánepa, *Historia general de la gran familia humana* (Buenos Aires, 1937), 147; Ramon Peyton Coffman and Nathan G. Goodman, *Famous Explorers for Boys and Girls* (New York, 1942), 21; *Encyclopedia Britannica* (London, Chicago, and New York, 1947), vol. 6, 79; and vol. 10, 146; Alberta Powell Graham, *Christopher Columbus, Discoverer* (New York, 1950), 21; Ingridel and Edgar Parin d'Aulaire, *Columbus* (New York, 1955), 7; Bernardine Bailey, *Christopher Columbus: Sailor and Dreamer* (Boston, 1960), 44; T*he American People: A History* (Arlington Heights, Ill., 1981).

7. *America Past and Present* (Scott Foresman, 1983), 98.

8. *We the People* (Heath, 1982), 28–29.

9. Crane Brinton, John Christopher, and Robert Wolff, *A History of Civilization: Prehistory to 1715* (Prentice-Hall). The account is found in the 1960 ed., 575; 1971 ed., 513; 1976 ed., 551.

10. Joseph Chiari, *Christopher Columbus* (New York, 1979).

11. School texts presenting correct accounts include *American History* (Allyn and Bacon, 1983), 24; *United States History* (Addison-Wellesley, 1986), 13; *The Rise of the American Nation* (Harcourt Brace Jovanovich, 1982), 12; *American Adventures* (Steck-Vaughan, 1987), 16. Encyclopedias presenting the correct account include *The New Encyclopedia Britannica* (1985); *Colliers Encyclopedia* (1984); *The Encyclopedia Americana* (1987); and T*he World Book for Children* (1989), which says, bluntly but rightly: "Columbus was not trying to 'prove the world was round,' as so often has been said. He didn't have to."

12. Daniel Boorstin, T*he Discoverers* (New York, 1983), 100.

13. Ibid., 109.

14. See chapter three in this book.

15. Charles E. Nowell, "The Columbus Question," *American Historical Review* 44 (1939): 802–22.

16. *Geography: An International Gallup Survey* (Princeton, N.J., 1988); see *Readers' Digest,* Feb. 1988 (132: 119–121); *Newsweek* (July 2, 1984 (104: 12) and Aug. 8, 1988 (112: 31); *Los Angeles Times,* Nov. 17, 1987 (I, 3:2) and Nov. 19, 1987 (II, 8:1); *US News and World Report,* Aug. 8, 1988 (105: 11).

17. Latin was the language of scholarship in Western Europe for the first seventeen centuries of our era. The ancient and medieval meanings of the key Latin words are ambiguous: *orbis* or *orbis terrarum* ("orb" or "orb of lands") could mean round in the full sense or merely circular (modern languages are also ambiguous, as in the English "round table"). *Rotundus,* too, may mean spherical or merely circular: it derives from *rota,* a wheel. The words *globus* and *sphaera* are sharper. A *globus* is sometimes an undifferentiated mass — a "glob" — but more often a ball, sphere, or orbit, and a *sphaera* is a ball or globe in addition to being a perfect geometrical figure.

18. James Johonnot, compiler and arranger, *Ten Great Events in History* (New York, 1887), 123–30.

19. Bartolomé de las Casas, *Historia de las Indias,* 3 vols. (written about 1560; ed. Gonzalo de Reparaz, Madrid, 1927), which contains an abstract of Columbus's own *Journal*; C. Columbus, *Journal of the First Voyage to America,* ed. Van Wyck Brooks (New York, 1924); Oliver Dunn and James E. Kelley Jr., *The Diario of Christopher Columbus's First Voyage to America 1492–1493 Abstracted by Fray Bartolomé de las Casas* (Norman, Okla., 1989); Ferdinand Columbus, *Historia del almirante* (1571) (I use the translation by Benjamin Keen, *The Life of the Admiral Christopher Columbus by His Son Ferdinand* [New Brunswick, N.J., 1959]); Pietro Martire d'Anghiera (1457–1526), *Decadas del nuevo mundo* (Buenos Aires, 1944). For Rodrigo Maldonado's account in 1515 of the meeting of the commission at Salamanca, see Samuel Eliot Morison, *Admiral of the Ocean Sea* (Boston, 1942), 88; and Alexander Geraldini's alleged eyewitness account of Salamanca written in 1520–1524 but not published until much later: *Itinerarium ad regiones sub aequinoctiali plaga constitutas* (Rome, 1631). See W. G. L. Randles, *De la terre plate au globe terrestre* (Paris, 1980), 29. Useful secondary sources are George Nunn, *The Geographical Conceptions of Columbus: A Critical Consideration of Four Problems* (New York, 1924), Felipe Fernandez-Armesto, *Columbus and the Conquest of the Impossible* (New York, 1974), Jacques Heers, *Christophe Colombe* (Paris, 1981), Cecil Jane, *Select Documents Illustrating the Four Voyages of Columbus*, 2 vols. (London, 1930–1933), and above all Morison, *Admiral* and *The European Discovery of America: The Southern Voyages* (New York, 1974). Morison's masterpieces checked the Flat Error's current but did not stop its flow. A popular, literary account was Salvador de Madariaga, *Christopher Columbus: Being the Life of the Very Magnificent Lord Don Cristobal Colon* (New York, 1940).

20. Columbus used a 1485 Latin translation of *The Book of Marco Polo,* an Italian translation of Pliny's *Natural History* printed in 1489, Pierre d'Ailly's *Imago mundi* published between 1480 and 1483, and a 1477 edition of Aeneas Silvius Piccolomini's *Historia rerum ubique gestarum.* Morison, *Admiral,* 92.

21. Ferdinand Columbus, *The Life of the Admiral,* chapters 6–7.

22. See Fidel Fernandez, *Fray Hernando de Talavera: Confesor de los reyes catolicos y primer arzobispo de Granada* (Madrid, 1942).

23. This objection may derive from "Sir John Mandeville" in the fourteenth century, who wrote of traveling "up" or "down" the sphere: see chapter three.

24. Morison, *Admiral,* 97–98. Heers, *Christophe Columb,* 190–91, offers a detailed refutation of the picture of the young hero facing the ignorant council. Heers makes an interesting suggestion: Irving may have been reading the Galileo case into that of Columbus.

25. Modern geographers know, but navigators then did not, that the earth is slightly larger East-West than North-South; in any event the difference is inconsiderable for navigational purposes. Not until the mid-eighteenth century was it possible to measure nautical distances with precision.

26. It also extended from 63 degrees North to 16 degrees South.

27. D'Ailly followed Marinus in his *Cosmographiae tractatus.* By modern calculations, Ptolemy's oikoumene, from the tip of Iberia to the tip of Siberia, spans about 200 degrees, so Marinus was in fact closer to the mark than Ptolemy. Marinus (c. A.D. 140) was an older contemporary of Ptolemy.

28. Columbus was influenced by his reading of the apocryphal book 4 Esdras (or 2 Esdras in most editions of the apocrypha) 6:42 to believe that the earth was six-sevenths land. Morison, *Admiral,* 71.

29. Alfragano's *Elementa astronomica* were translated from Arabic into Latin by Gerard of Cremona and Joannes Hispalensis in the twelfth century.

30. Morison gives a clear account of the politics and preparations in *Admiral,* 79–149.

31. Astronomers such as Georg Peurbach (1423–1461) and Regiomontanus (Johannes Müller, 1436–1476), assumed it. Authors of works on the sphere include Henry of Simbergh, Conrad de Monte Puellarum, Dominic de Chivasso, Andalo di Negro, Nicholas Oresme, and Pierre D'Ailly. The "Geography," (*Cosmographia*) of Ptolemy was translated into Latin from Greek in 1410 by Jacopo

d'Angelo. Aeneas Silvius Piccolomini (1405–1464) used it in his *Historia rerum ubique gestarum*. Aristotle's treatises "On the Heavens" and "Metaphysics" were translated in the twelfth and thirteenth centuries.

32. D'Ailly completed his *Imago mundi* about 1410 and later composed a *Compendium cosmographiae* summarizing Ptolemy's geography. Edmond Buron, *Ymago mundi de Pierre d'Ailly* (Paris, 1930). Columbus's own copy of D'Ailly is densely annotated.

33. Edward Grant, *Physical Science in the Middle Ages* (New York, 1971), 61. In 1496 Lilio published a strange book containing treatises on the wretchedness of the human lot, the nature of the winds, the life of Charlemagne, and the antipodes. Zacharia Lilio, *In hoc volumine continentur hi libri Zachariae Lilii. Primus liber: De origine et laudibus scientiarum; secundus liber: Contra Antipodes; tertius liber: De miseria hominis et contemptu mundi; quartus liber: De generibus ventorum; quintus liber: Vita Caroli Magni* (Florence, impressum per F. Bonacursum, in quarto, 1496). See Randles, *De la terre plate au globe terrestre*, 31. A perusal of the original text indicates Lilio's confusion, for he cites Ptolemy's measurement of the known world against the "roundness" of the earth. Alonso Tostado Ribera (d. 1455), "Commentaria in Genesim," in *Opera omnia* may be another anomaly.

34. Roger Bacon, *Opus maius* 4.4.10, trans. Robert Belle Burke, 2 vols. (Philadelphia, 1928). The *Opus maius*, which appeared in 1266, was a direct influence on D'Ailly. Bacon followed Albert the Great in affirming that the ocean could be crossed and the antipodes inhabited: see Albert, *De natura locorum*, ed. Auguste Borgnet (Paris, 1891), 1:6–12.

35. Jean Buridan, *Quaestiones super libris quattuor de caelo et mundo*, ed. E. A. Moody (Cambridge, Mass., 1942), 159. See Edward Grant, "Cosmology," in *Science in the Middle Ages*, ed. David Lindberg (Chicago, 1978), 284–91; Randles, *De la terre plate au globe terrestre*, 43. Randles offers the hypothesis that the disc-shaped medieval maps offer a roughly accurate picture of a small, flat oikoumene perched atop a globe of water, and indeed this fits the apparent view of writers such as Dicuil, who measured the length and breadth of a flat known world without attempting any spherical projection. Nicole Oresme, *Le livre du ciel et du monde*, ed. A. D. Menut and A. J. Denomy (Madison, 1968), 563–65.

36. *Mandeville's Travels: Texts and Translations*, ed. Malcolm Letts (London, 1953), including the English text (chapter 19: 128) for the stars and the French text (chapter 20: 331–34 for the argument).

"Pour quoy on peut (331) apperceuoir que la terre et 1a mer sont de ronde fourme; car la partie du firmament appartient a un pays qui ne appartient point a autre. Et ce peut-on apperceuoir par experience et subtille indicacion, que se on trouuoit passage de nef et gens qui vouissent aler et cerchier le monde, on pourroit aler a nauie tout entour le monde, et desseure et dessoubz. . . . (334): Il semble aus simples gens que on ne pourroit aler dessous la terre et que on deuroit cheoir vers le ciel, quant on seroit dessouz la terre. Mais ce ne pourroit estre, neent plus que nous pourrions cheoir vers le ciel de la terre ou nous sommes." (For this reason one can understand that the land and the sea are round in form, for the part of the sky that is over one country is not the same as that over another. And one can know this through experience and clever reasoning, for if one found a ship and sailors who wanted to go and see the world, one could go on a vessel all around the world, and above it and below it. It seems to simple people that one could not go below and that one would fall off towards the sky there. But that could not be, any more than we can fall off the earth into the sky from the part of the earth that we dwell in.)

37. William Caxton, *Mirrour of the World,* ed. Oliver H. Prior EETS #110 (Oxford, 1913, repr. 1966), 52. Prior, ed., *L'Image du monde de Maître Gossouin* (Lausanne, 1913). The text is no longer attributed to "Gossouin." The first verse redaction was 1246; a second, longer, verse version dates from 1248, and a prose version appeared probably in 1247.

38. Charles-Victor Langlois, *La Connaissance de la nature et du monde au moyen âge, d'après quelques écrits français à l'usage des laics* (Paris, 1911), 226. The thirteenth-century vernacular *South English Legendary* showed awareness of the earth's shape. See Albert Van Helden, *Measuring the Universe: Cosmic Dimensions from Aristarchus to Halley* (Chicago, 1985), 38. Buron, *Ymago mundi de Pierre d'Ailly,* 1:9 : "comme une mouche iroit entour une pomme reonde." The Ymago goes on to say that if you could throw a stone down a chute through the earth, it would stop at the center; the earth is almost a perfect sphere, and such features as mountains are insignificant compared with the whole. Brunetto Latini, *Livres dou tresor,* ed. F. J. Carmody (Berkeley, 1948). See Langlois, *La Connaissance,* 349; Jill Tattersall, "Sphere or Disc? Allusions to the Shape of the Earth in Some Twelfth-century and Thirteenth-century Vernacular French Works," *Modern Language Review* 76 (1981): 31–34. The eggshell image was common in the twelfth

through fourteenth centuries, as in Abelard, Peter Comestor, Gervase of Tilbury, Adelard of Bath, William of Conches, Daniel of Morley, Michael Scot, and Perot de Garbelei: see Tattersall, "Sphere or Disc?" Apples and balls were common images, as in the Anglo-Norman *Petite philosophie* (c. 1230), where lines 253, 359 call the earth "rund cume pelote," round as a ball; Tattersall, "Sphere or Disc?" 34–43, cites these and a variety of other French vernacular writers.

39. Béroul, *Tristan*, ed. A. Ewert (Oxford, 1939), lines 3379–80: "Ja verroiz le Table Ronde, /Qui tornoie comme le monde. Tattersall, 44, discusses this and other texts to demonstrate their muddle.

40. Tattersall, "Sphere or Disc?" 46.

41. Jeffrey B. Russell, *Lucifer* (Ithaca, N.Y., 1984), 216–33.

42. David Woodward, "Reality, Symbolism, Time, and Space in Medieval World Maps," *Annals of the Association of American Geographers*, 75 [4] (1985): 511.

43. Woodward, "Reality, Symbolism, Time, and Space," 511, gives four categories: tripartite, zonal, quadripartite, and transitional.

44. Compare a modern map of "the polar regions."

45. Von den Brincken, "Die Kugelgestalt der Erde in der Kartographie des Mittelalters," 85, estimates that 99 of 636 maps she surveyed were efforts at projection.

46. Ezekiel 5:5: "I have set the city of Jerusalem in the midst of the nations and their peoples."

47. See Woodward, "Reality, Symbolism, Time, and Space," 519; Jane, *Select Documents*, 56; Randles, *De la terre plate au globe terrestre*, 20; Edward Grant, "Cosmology," in *Science in the Middle Ages*, David C. Lindberg (Chicago, 1978), 266; P.D.A. Harvey, "Medieval Maps," in *The History of Cartography: Cartography in Prehistoric, Ancient, and Medieval Europe and the Mediterranean*, J. B. Harley and David C. Woodward (Chicago, 1987), 284. Woodward, "Medieval *Mappaemundi*" in *The History of Cartography*, Harley and Woodward, 297 illustrates the four major types of *mappaemundi*.

48. See Lynn Thorndike, ed. and trans., *Joannes de Sacrobosco: The Sphere of Sacrobosco and Its Commentators* (Chicago, 1949), 81–83 and 120, and the commentaries by Michael Scot (294–95) and Cecco d'Ascoli (366–67). Sacrobosco, 81: "Quod terra etiam sit rotunda sic patet (Thus it is clear that the earth is round.)." Sacrobosco received commentaries from Michael Scot, Robert the Englishman, and Cecco

d'Ascoli. Campanus of Novara's *Theorica planetarum* (about 1260) was more advanced and detailed.

49. Notable are Thabit ibn Qurra (827–901), al-Biruni (973–1048), al-Urdi (d. 1266), and al-Farghani (800–870). These were translated into Latin in the twelfth century. The Arabs had translated Ptolemy's *Almagest* (its Arabic name) into Arabic in the ninth century.

50. Aquinas, *Summa theologiae* Ia: q68 a2; Aquinas, *De coelo et mundo* 2:28; Aquinas, *Commentarium in II Sententiarum:* "rotunditas terrae," etc. Adelard, *Quaestiones naturales,* 48–49; Adelard, *Expositio in Hexaemeron,* MPL 178, 735–48; Honorius Augustodensis, *De imagine mundi libri tres* (MPL 172, 121–22); Hermann von Reichenau. *De utilitatibus astrolabii,* chapters 2–4 (MPL 143:408–10); Alexander Neckham, *De natura rerum* (Rolls Series: 34), 1:5, 2:14; Geoffrey of Viterbo, *Pantheon* (MGH SS 22, 274–75); Lambert of St Omer, *Liber floridus* (MPL 163); Petrus Alfonsi, *De philosophia mundi libri quatuor* (MPL 172); Petrus Alfonsi, *Dragmaticon philosophiae* (MPL 172 under Honorius); Robert Grosseteste, *De sphaera*; Gervase of Tilbury, *Otia imperialia,* ed. F. Liebrecht (Hanover, 1856), 885 (ambiguous); Hildegarde of Bingen, *Scivias* 1:3; Hildegarde, *Liber de operatione Dei:* 1:2–4; Albertus Magnus, *De coelo et mundo*: 2:4.9–11; William of Conches, *De philosophia mundi* 4:2–3.

51. Cassiodorus even recommends the study of Ptolemy to his monks in *De artibus ac disciplinis liberalium litterarum* (MPL 70). Writers alluding to sphericity include Avitus (died c. 520), *De spiritalis historiae gestis* 1:53; Macrobius, *Commentarii in somnium Scipionis* 1:20, in *Macrobe: Oeuvres complètes* (Paris, 1883); Martianus Capella, *Martianus Capella and the Seven Liberal Arts,* vol. 2: *The Marriage of Philology and Mercury,* ed. James Willis (Leipzig, 1983), trans. William Harris Stahl and Richard Johnson, 218–24, 318, 330–34. Of the one exception, Cosmas Indicopleustes, see later chapters. See Van Helden, *Measuring the Universe,* 27.

52. Martianus, *Martianus Capella* 220–24: "non planam . . . neque concavam . . . sed rotundam, globosam etiam." Macrobius, like Crates, believed that the inhabited world was a small island on a vast globe of sea.

53. Isidore used the term *globus* for the moon and planets; he spoke of the axis of the celestial sphere. See Isidore, *Etymologies*: 3:27–53; 13:1–6; 14:1–2. Book 3:40–41 is very confused, and 3:47

makes the perverse observation that the sun rises in the east at the same time as it rises in the west. In his *De natura rerum*, ed. Jacques Fontaine, *Isidore de Seville: Traité de la nature* (Bordeaux, 1960), chapter 16 duplicates this error, but chapter 28 says, to the contrary, that the sun orbits the earth and illumines the other side when it is night on this side. In chapter 48 Isidore estimates the circumference of the earth at 80,000 stadia (see also chapters 10–14; 45). *Etymologies* 3:32 and 14:1 affirm that the sphere of the sky is round with the earth at its center, the sky being equally distant from the earth on all sides. See Olaf Pedersen, "Astronomy," in Lindberg, *Science*, 307; Woodward in *The History of Cartography*, Harley and Woodward, 320: "Despite Isidore's apparent confusion . . . the evidence appears to confirm that he thought the earth, like the universe, was a sphere."

54. Jeffrey B. Russell, "Saint Boniface and the Eccentrics," *Church History* 33 (1964):235–47.

55. Bede, *De natura rerum,* chapters 3, 5, 6–10, 36–39, 46: "We call the earth a globe, not as if the shape of a sphere were expressed in the diversity of plains and mountains, but because, if all things are included in the outline, the earth's circumference will represent the figure of a perfect globe" (46). Bede, *Bedae opera de temporibus*, ed. C. W. Jones (Cambridge, Mass., 1943), chapter 32: "Causa autem inaequalitatis eorundem dierum terrae rotunditas est; neque enim frustra et in scripturae divinae et in communium litterarum paginis orbis terrae vocatur. Est enim re vera orbis idem in medio totius mundi positus, non in latitudinis solum giro quasi instar scuti rotundus sed instar potius pilae undique versum aequali rotunditate persimilis." (The cause of the inequality of the length of days is that the earth is round, and it is not in vain that in both the bible and pagan literature it is called the "orb of lands." For truly it is an orb placed in the center of the universe; in its width it is like a circle, and not circular like a shield but rather like a ball, and it extends from its center with perfect roundness on all sides.) A much later compatriot of Bede's, the monk Byrhtferth of Ramsey abbey in the eleventh century, upheld the idea in his *Manual*, ed. EETS 177 (1929): 80–81, 124–25. Eriugena, *Periphyseon,* trans. I. P. Sheldon-Williams, Rev. John O'Meara (Montreal, 1987), 347–53. Eriugena describes how the Greek Eratosthenes had calculated the circumference of the globe.

56. Raban Maur, *De universo* (MPL 111: 332–33). His *Liber de computo* (MPL 107) is clearer: in chapters 46–50 he uses terms such as

globo terrae and *globo terrarum*. Gerbert (Pope Sylvester II, 945–1003), *Liber de astrolabe* in *Opera mathematica*, ed. Nicholas Bubnov (Berlin, 1899); Gerbert was influenced by Martianus Capella. Dicuil (9th century), *Liber de mensura orbis terrae*, ed. J. J. Tierney (Dublin, 1967), measures the length and breadth of a flat *orbis terrae* but clearly refers to the oikoumene ("Europa, Asia, Libya"). Alcuin made no explicit statement on the topic but regarded Pliny and Bede as authorities.

57. Damascene, *On the Orthodox Faith (De fide orthodoxa)*, 2:6. Basil, *Hexaemeron*, Sources chrétiennes 26 (1949), 126–29; 480–83.

58. The "literal" interpretation of the Bible is much spoken of and little understood. Since any text can be (and is inevitably) read in a variety of ways, the only useful sense of "literal" is the original intent of the author, which is often difficult to discern. Even the most avid "literalists," however, must see the difference between poetic and historical statements.

59. See also Deuteronomy 5:8; 13:7; 28:64; 33:17; I Samuel 2:10; Psalms 48:10; 61:2; 65:5; 88(89):11–12; 98:3; 103(104):3; 135; Proverbs 17:24; 30:4; Isaiah 5:2; 11:2; Jeremiah 25:33; Job 37:3; Ezekiel 7:2; Revelation 7:1; 20:8. Most of these have to do with "quarters" of the earth (which can be understood in either flat or round terms) or "ends" of the earth, the kind of passages that Augustine took metaphorically. For example Proverbs 30:4, speaking of God, says, "Who has mounted to the heavens, then descended? who has gathered the wind in the clasp of his hand? who has wrapped the waters in his cloak? who has set all the ends of the earth firm?" How can one insist that this means that the earth physically has "ends" without insisting that God wraps the ocean in a physical cloak?

60. Isaiah 40:22. The Greek uses the term *ho gyros* for the earth, which more likely means "circle" than "sphere," and says that God ho stesas hos kamaran ton ouranon, kai diateinas hos skenen katoikein; the Vulgate renders this as Qui sedet super gyrum terrae . . . qui extendit velut nihilum coelos, et expandit eos sicut tabernaculum ad inhabitandum (He who sits above the circle of the earth, who extends the skies as a void and expands them like a tent for us to inhabit.); Job 22:14; Amos 9:6; Psalm 104:2.

61. Augustine, *De genesi ad litteram*: 1:9–10; 1:19; 1:21; 2:9. Augustine, *The Literal Meaning of Genesis*, ed. and trans. John Hammond Taylor, 2 vols. (New York 1982), 1: 42–43, 58–60. Augustine, *Confessions*, 11:23; 13:15.

62. Augustine, *City of God*, 16:9.

63. Ambrose, *Hexaemeron libri sex*, 1:3; 2:3. See also Origen's *Homilies on Genesis* (Sources chrétiennes 7, 1943); Gregory of Nyssa, *In Hexaemeron explicatio apologetica* (MPG 44); Chrysostom's *Homilies and Sermons on Genesis*. See Pierre Duhem, *Le système du monde* (Paris, 10 vols., 1913–59), vol. 2, part 2, chapter 1: "La cosmologie des pères de l'église," 393–95. Eusebius of Caesarea, (*Praeparatio evangelica* (MPL 21), 15:56–57) sorts through the opinions of the philosophers and seems to opt for roundness: 15:56–57.

64. Photius and John Philoponus (c. 490–570) seem to imply this while rejecting the opinion. Charles Raymond Beazley, *The Dawn of Modern Geography*, 3 vols. (London, 1897–1906), 1:351–52.

65. Photius, *Myriobiblon sive bibliotheca* (MPG 103: 829–77). For vaults see Job 22:14; Amos 9:6.

66. Severian, *In cosmogoniam homiliae*, 3:4–5 in MPG 56:452–53.

67. W. M. O'Neil, *Early Astronomy from Babylonia to Copernicus* (Sydney, 1986).

68. D. R. Dicks, *Early Greek Astronomy to Aristotle* (Ithaca, N.Y., 1970), 72.

69. Ibid., 72–198; Thomas S. Kuhn, *The Copernican Revolution* (Cambridge, Mass., 1957), 26–85; Heraclides of Pontus also suggested that the apparent motion of the stars was caused by the actual rotation of the earth, and Aristarchus argued for a heliocentric universe. See also van Helden, *Measuring the Universe*, 4–15 and Harold P. Nebelsick, *Circles of God: Theology and Science from the Greeks to Copernicus* (Edinburgh, 1985), 9–51.

70. Kuhn, *The Copernican Revolution*, 85.

71. Germaine Aujac, "The Growth of an Empirical Cartography in Hellenistic Greece," in *The History of Cartography*, Harley and Woodward, 156.

72. Ibid., 157.

73. On Crates, Hipparchus, Theodosius of Bithynia (c. 150–70 B.C.), Posidonius (c. 135–50 B.C.), Geminus of Rhodes (c. 70 B.C.), Strabo, and Marinus of Tyre (c. A.D. 100) see *The History of Cartography*, Harley and Woodward, 161–255. Harley, 174: Strabo knew from Eratosthenes how to project a sphere upon a plane surface.

74. On Ptolemy see O.A.W. Dilke, "The Culmination of Greek Cartography in Ptolemy," in *The History of Cartography*, Harley and Woodward, 177–200. Unlike Strabo's, Ptolemy's map erred in enclosing the Indian Ocean.

75. Pomponius Mela, *De situ orbis libri tres*, 3 vols. (Leipzig,

1806–1807), 1:1. *De situ orbis* speaks of the "antichthones" who live opposite us; we cannot get to them because the torrid zone south of the equator is too hot.

76. Boorstin, *The Discoverers*, 102.

77. Jan Ryder helped both in identifying some of the modern proponents of the Error and later in reading over the whole manuscript; I am greatly in her debt.

78. Boorstin, *The Discoverers*, 146–49.

79. Andrew Dickson White, *A History of the Warfare of Science with Theology in Christendom,* 2 vols. (New York, 1896), 1:97. The only sense to be made out of the opening into hell is the legend that (because of its intense volcanic activity) the area around Iceland opened into the underworld. It is also true that the Greeks and the Romans feared the seas beyond the Straits of Gibraltar owing to the vastness and bad climate of the Atlantic, so that it had a fearsomely numinous aura to it. Nonetheless, the numinous power of the Ocean did not prevent ancient Greeks, Phoenicians, and Romans, as well as their medieval successors, from plying the western coasts of Europe for trade.

80. A. Holt-Jensen, *Geography: Its History and Concepts, A Student's Guide,* 2d ed. (London, 1988), 12–13.

81. F. S. Marvin, "Science and the Unity of Mankind," in *Studies in the History and Method of Science*, ed. Charles Singer, 2 vols., 2d ed. (London 1921), 2:352. See also G. Pouchet, *Histoire des sciences naturelles au moyen âge* (Paris, 1853), 490.

82. M. E. Thalheimer, *The Eclectic History of the United States* (Cincinnati, 1881), 23.

83. Joachim Lelewel, *Géographie du moyen âge,* 4 vols. (Brussels, 1850–1852), 1:lxxvii–lxxix.

84. The Cubberley Library in the Stanford University School of Education houses a collection of old textbooks; I checked all that were relevant and found that a large number of texts before 1870 do not even allude to the controversy; after 1880 most make the flat-earth accusation. Monsieur Campe, *La découverte de l'Amérique: Pour l'instruction et l'amusement des jeunes gens* (Geneva, 1798; Brunswick, 1811) suggests that the question arose at the time of Columbus; C. O. Barbaroux, *L'histoire des Etats-unis de l'Amérique* (Boston, 1832): no mention; Joseph E. Worcester, *Elements of History* (Boston, 1850): the question arose, and "Columbus had more correct ideas of the figure of the earth than were common in his time;" Jacob Abbott, *American His-*

tory (New York, 1860–1865): no mention; G. P. Quackenbos, *Illustrated School History of the United States of America* (New York, 1872): "The geographical researches of Columbus had convinced him that the earth was round;" Edward A. Freeman, *Outlines of History* (New York, 1873) skirts the issue; *A Primary History of the United States* (New York, 1885, anon.): people thought Columbus was crazy, but the enlightened Queen Isabella believed him [the same enlightened Queen Isabella that established the Spanish Inquisition!]; Thomas Wentworth Higgins, *Young Folks' History of the United States* (London and New York, 1898): "Most persons" believed the earth was flat. Dates of other texts making no mention: 1828, 1832, 1855, 1866, 1868, 1869.

85. Bishop Davenport, *History of the United States* (Philadelphia, 1831), 6; Emma Willard, *Abridged History of the United States* (New York, 1846), 22.

86. Herder (1744–1803) and Goethe (1749–1832), among other popular and influential writers, had romantically positive views of the Middle Ages.

87. J. B. Bury, *The Idea of Progress* (London, 1920), 30.

88. Jules Michelet, *Histoire de France* (Paris, 1876), 7: 7–11; 37.

89. W.E.H. Lecky, *Rationalism in Europe*, 2 vols. (New York, 1867), 1:275–80. See Charles Kingsley, *Scientific Lectures and Essays* (London, 1880).

90. I. Todhunter, *William Whewell D.D.: Master of Trinity College, Cambridge* (London, 1876; repr. 2 vols., New York, 1970), 1:411. On Whewell's character, 1:415 and throughout.

91. William Whewell, *History of the Inductive Sciences from the Earliest to the Present Time*, 3 vols. (London, 1837). I used 3d ed. 2 vols. New York, 1897. On the Middle Ages: 1:185; on the antipodes: 1:196 (here he correctly distinguishes between the question of the antipodes and that of sphericity but then immediately allows his rhetoric to carry him into blurring the two). On Lactantius and Cosmas: 1:195–97. For a list of sixteenth-century authors attacking Lactantius, see Randles, *De la terre plate au globe terrestre*, 88–90.

92. On Lactantius see Jeffrey B. Russell, *Satan* (Ithaca, N.Y., 1981), 149–59. Randles, *De la terre plate au globe terrestre*, 14, notes how modern historians have belabored Lactantius as a "perfect example of an obtuse and reactionary mind." The relevant passages are in Lactantius, *De divinis institutionibus*, 3:3; 3:24.

93. Isaiah 40:22, Matthew 24:31; Revelation 7:1. On Cosmas see

Germaine Aujac, "The Foundations of Theoretical Cartography in Archaic and Classical Greece, in *The History of Cartography*, Harley and Woodward, 144, and O.A.W. Dilke, "Cartography in the Byzantine Empire," in *The History of Cartography*, Harley and Woodward, 261–63. The standard works are by Wanda Wolska-Conus, ed., *Cosmas Indicopleustes*, Sources chrétiennes, 141 (1968), 159 (1970), 197 (1973); Wolska-Conus, *La topographie chrétienne de Cosmas Indicopleustès: Théologie et science au VIe siècle* (Paris, 1962). Cosmas was first edited by Bernard de Montfaucon in 1706; the first modern edition of the *Christianike topographia* was by E. O. Winstedt, *The Christian Topography of Cosmas Indicopleustes* (Cambridge, 1909), after J. W. McCrindle's text and commentary, *The Christian Topography of Cosmas, an Egyptian Monk* (London, 1897).

94. Wolska-Conus, ed., *Cosmas Indicopleustes*, prologue 2, 1: 258–59.

95. Ibid., 2:79–80, 394–99. Apparently, Cosmas himself claims to have derived his ideas from *The History of Ephorus* (405–330 B.C.), a work now lost.

96. Origen, *Homilies on Exodus*, 9:4. See Wolska-Conus, *La Topographie*, 116.

97. Wolska-Conus, ed., *Cosmas Indicopleustes* prologue 4–6; 1:14; 2:17; 3:51; 4:15. The idea that the sun was hidden at night by high mountains in the far north was put forward by Anaximenes and cited as an opinion by Aristotle, *Meteorologica*, 2:1, ed. H. D. P. Lee (Cambridge, Mass., 1952), 128–30. See J. Oliver Thomson, *History of Ancient Geography* (Cambridge, 1948), 36.

98. Wolska-Conus, *La Topographie*, 30. Wolska-Conus, ed., *Cosmas Indicopleustes*, 1:14, 2:107, 4:22–24.

99. Dilke in *The History of Cartography*, Harley and Woodward, 263; Winstedt, *The Christian Topography of Cosmas Indicopleustes*, 15–32.

100. Wolska-Conus, *La Topographie,* 149. Underlying the philosophical differencc was a political/theological animosity, because Philoponus was a Monophysite and Cosmas a Chalcedonian. John Philoponus, *Against Aristotle, on the Eternity of the World*, trans. Christian Wildberg (Ithaca, N.Y., 1987).

101. Bernard de Montfaucon, ed., *Nova collectio patrum et scriptorum graecorum* (1706), reproduced in MPG 88.

102. Woodward, "Medieval *Mappaemundi*," in *The History of Cartography*, Harley and Woodward, 319. A copy of the "Christian Topogra-

phy" in Greek "has been traced to the early medieval Cathedral Library in York." Walter Berschin, *Greek Letters and the Latin Middle Ages: From Jerome to Nicholas of Cusa* (Washington, D.C., 1988), 37. Philip Grierson, "The European Heritage," in *Ancient Cosmologies*, ed. Carmen Blacker and Michael Loewe (London, 1975), 237.

103. J. W. McCrindle, *The Christian Topography of Cosmas, an Egyptian monk,* trans. and ed. J. W. McCrindle (London, 1897). McCrindle's bias makes itself felt immediately in the Preface: Cosmas's work appears "at that period in the world's history, when Christendom, fast losing the light of Greek learning and culture, was soon to be shrouded in the long night of mediaeval ignorance and barbarism."

104. John Herman Randall, Jr., *The Making of the Modern Mind* (Boston, 1926; Cambridge, Mass., 1940), 23. George H. T. Kimble, *Geography in the Middle Ages* (London, 1938), 35.

105. David Lindberg and Ronald Numbers, *God and Nature* (Berkeley, 1986).

106. John W. Draper, *History of the Intellectual Development of Europe* (New York and London, 1863); Draper, *History of the Conflict Between Religion and Science* (New York, 1874). James R. Moore, *The Post-Darwinian Controversies* (Cambridge, 1979), 26; Donald Fleming, *John William Draper and the Religion of Science* (Philadelphia, 1950).

107. The importance of the confrontation may be exaggerated. See J. R. Lucas, "Wilberforce and Huxley: A Legendary Encounter," *The Historical Journal* 22 (1979): 313–30.

108. Moore, *The Post-Darwinian Controversies*, 60–61, pointed out that the Wilberforce-Huxley confrontation became a symbol of a declaration of war in the minds of later polemicists.

109. Fleming, *John William Draper*, 89.

110. The English and their American descendants painted Spain as a fearsome land of bigotry and persecution, Catholic and reactionary, inherently inclined to the suppression of truth. See Sverker Arnoldsson, *La leyenda negra: Estudios sobre sus origines* (Stockholm, 1960); Philip W. Powell, *The Tree of Hate: Propaganda and Prejudices Affecting United States Relations with the Hispanic World* (New York, 1971); Charles Gibson, *The Black Legend: Anti-Spanish Attitudes in the Old World and the New* (New York, 1971); Julian Juderías, *La leyenda negra: Estudios acerca del concepto de España en el extranjero,* 16th ed. (Madrid, 1974).

111. Draper, *History of the Conflict*, 363.

112. Ibid., vi–vii.

113. Ibid., xi.

114. Ibid., 62.

115. Ibid., 160.

116. The words are taken verbatim from Washington Irving, *The Life and Voyages of Christopher Columbus* (Boston, 1981), 48–49.

117. Draper, *History of the Conflict*, 65, places St. Bede in the wrong century. On the fathers: 56–64; on the scholastics: 150; on Columbus: 160–61.

118. P.V.N. Myers, *A General History for Colleges and High Schools* (Boston and London, 1891), 513.

119. Andrew Dickson White, *A History of the Warfare of Science with Theology in Christendom*, 2 vols. (New York, 1896). See White, *The Autobiography of Andrew Dickson White* (New York, 1905); Glenn C. Altschuler, *Andrew Dickson White: Educator, Historian, Diplomat* (Ithaca, N.Y., 1979), 202–16.

120. Lindberg and Numbers, "Beyond War and Peace," 339.

121. White, *History of the Warfare*, 1:113.

122. Ibid., 1:91.

123. Konrad Kretschmer, *Die Entdeckung Amerika's in ihrer Bedeutung für die Geschichte des Weltbildes* (Berlin, 1892).

124. White, *History of the Warfare*, 1:92.

125 Lindberg and Numbers, "Beyond War," 342.

126. White, *History of the Warfare*, 1:92.

127. Ibid., 1:91–92; on Cosmas: 1:93–95; on Lactantius: 1:97; on the Middle Ages: 1:105–6; on Gerbert and Bacon: 1:110–11. It is true that legend (never theology) made Gerbert and Roger Bacon wizards, but hardly because they calculated the earth's circumference. White may have had sorcery on the brain because of the research of his assistant and collaborator George Lincoln Burr into witchcraft. But Burr's own lecture "Anent the Middle Ages," in *George Lincoln Burr: His Life; Selections from his Writings*, ed. Roland Bainton, 2 vols. (Ithaca, 1943), 378–96, is too careful and judicious to mention the Flat Error.

128. White, *History of the Warfare*, 1:108–9. White follows this statement by an irrelevant reference to Alexander VI's division of the world between Portugal and Spain.

129. Lindberg and Numbers, "Beyond War," 338–40.

130. Ibid., "Beyond War," 352–54.

131. Less rigid: George Burton Adams, *Civilization during the Middle*

Ages (1883); John Tyndall, *Fragments of Science,* 7th ed., 2 vols. (London, 1889), 2:146–47; rigid: John Fiske, *The Discovery of America,* 2 vols. (Boston, 1892), 266; Konrad Kretschmer, *Die Entdeckung Amerika's in ihrer Bedeutung fuer die Geschichte des Weltbildes* (Berlin, 1892), 92–93; Henry Hallam, *View of the State of Europe During the Middle Ages,* 3 vols. (London, 1878). See Moore, *The Post-Darwinian Controversies,* 40–46.

132. Sigmund Günther, *Das Zeitalter der Entdeckungen,* 3d ed. (Leipzig, 1912), 6, 41.

133. J. H. Parry, *The Discovery of the Sea* (London, 1974), 58.

134. Maynard Shipley, *The War on Modern Science* (New York and London, 1927), 3.

135. O'Neil, *Early Astronomy from Babylonia to Copernicus,* 101–2. Gianni Gransotto, *Christopher Columbus* (Garden City, N.Y., 1985), 50, offers the really idiosyncratic view that medieval people thought the sea was "infinite." Compare Harold Lamb, *New Found World: How North America Was Discovered and Explored* (New York, 1955), 39.

136. Boorstin, *The Discoverers,* 102.

137. Ibid., 107–9.

138. Fleming, *John William Draper,* 131–32.

139. Boorstin, *The Discoverers,* 688–89.

140. James Young Simpson, *Landmarks in the Struggle Between Science and Religion* (London, 1925); John Kirtland Wright, *The Geographical Lore of the Time of the Crusades* (New York, 1925); George H. T. Kimble, *Geography in the Middle Ages* (London, 1938); see also A. Pannekoek, *A History of Astronomy* (New York, 1961): 173–77.

141. Simpson, *Landmarks in the Struggle,* 97.

142. Wright: *Geographical Lore,* 53–54; F. S. Betten, "Knowledge of the Sphericity of the Earth During the Earlier Middle Ages," *Catholic Historical Review* 3 (1923): 74–90.

143. Kimble, *Geography in the Middle Age,* 19, 36.

144. Charles Raymond Beazley, *The Dawn of Modern Geography,* 3 vols. (London, 1897–1906), 1:39, 44–46, 274–75, 329.

145. Washington Irving, *The Life and Voyages of Christopher Columbus,* ed. John Harmon McElroy (Boston, 1981), 50; Anderson merely changed Irving's "antipodes:" to "people." John J. Anderson, *Popular History of the United States* (New York, 1880), 19; Anderson, *New Grammar School History of the United States* (New York, 1898), 21. Among other schoolbooks deriving directly from Irving are *Tales from American*

History (New York, 1833); Henry Altemus, *Christopher Columbus and the Discovery of America* (Philadelphia, 1897).

146. Washington Irving, *A History of New York,* ed. Michael L. Black and Nancy B. Black (Boston, 1984).

147. Ibid., 3–4.

148. Irving embellished his account with pseudo-footnotes, for example p. 22, where the reference is simply "Mss. Bibliot. Roi. Fr.," a useless, untraceable reference to unspecified "manuscripts in the French royal library." Moreover, the reference is to the adventures of a luridly fictitious "Aboul-Hassan-Aly." Nancy Partner, "Making Up Lost Time: Writing on the Writing of History," *Speculum* 61 (1986): 90–117, demonstrates that there is no clear borderline between history and fiction. All fiction is about real human beings in at least the sense that it draws upon the author's experience of humans, and all history involves creative acts of organization, choice of point of view, choice of sources, and human empathy as well as literary composition. Honesty and respect for one's audience demand only that the author be frank about his intention and his assumptions.

149. Irving, *Columbus*, 47–51.

150. Morison, *Admiral*, 88–89. Antonio de Herrera de Tordesillas, *Historia general de los hechos de los Castellanos en las Islas i Tierra Firma del mar oceano* (Madrid, 1601–1615).

151. Salvador de Madariaga, *Vida del muy magnifico señor Don Cristobal Colon*, 7th ed. (Buenos Aires, 1959), 219.

152. Gonzalo Fernandez de Oviedo y Valdes, *Historia general y natural de las Indias*, 4 vols. (Madrid, 1851–1855) 1:18–20; Irving cites book 2, chapter 4. Ferdinand Columbus, *The Life of the Admiral*, chapters 6–7. Antonio de Remesal, *Historia general de las Indias occidentales y particular de la gobernacion de Chiapa y Guatemala* (Madrid, 1619); Bartolomé de las Casas, *Historia de las Indias*, 3 vols. (Madrid, 1927), *History of the Indies* ed. and trans. Andrée Collard (New York, 1971). The original is: "Como todo el agua y la tierra del mundo constituyen una esfera y, par consiguiente, sea redondo, consideró Cristóbal Colón ser posible rodearse de Oriente a Occidente" (Since all the water and land of the earth constitute a sphere and consequently are round, Christopher Columbus considered it possible to travel east to west.) Irving also used Antonio de Herrera, *The General History of America,* trans. John Stevens (London, 1725–1726) and Juan B. Muñoz, *Historia del Nuevo-Mundo* (Madrid, 1793). On Irving's use of the sources on Salamanca, see Madariaga, *Vida del muy magnifico*, 215–16.

153. Heers, *Christophe Columb*, 190. Madariaga, *Vida del muy magnifico*, 215–16. Madariaga confirms that neither Ferdinand Columbus nor Las Casas mention anything to do with the flat earth. Note, too, that as against some modern accounts, Talavera was not archbishop of Granada until 1487, although in 1486 he was already influential as Queen Isabella's confessor.

154. Martin Fernandez de Navarrete, *Colección de los viajes y descubrimientos que hicieron por mar los Españoles desde fines del siglo xv*, 5 vols. (Madrid, 1825–1837); vols. 1–2 (1825) pertain to Columbus. None mentions the alleged council of Salamanca. See Jeffrey Rubin-Dorsky, *Adrift in the Old World: The Psychological Pilgrimage of Washington Irving* (Chicago, 1988), 219–23.

155. Rubin-Dorsky, *Adrift in the Old World*, 221.

156. Irving to Pierre Irving, quoted by McElroy, *Life and Voyages*, lxxv.

157. Edward Wagenknecht, *Washington Irving: Moderation Displayed* (New York, 1962), 182–85; see also Mary Weatherspoon Bowden, *Washington Irving* (Boston, 1981).

158. Wagenknecht, *Washington Irving: Moderation Displayed*, 184.

159. William Hedges, *Washington Irving: An American Study, 1802–1832*; (Baltimore, 1965), 241.

160. Quoted by Wagenknecht, *Washington Irving: Moderation Displayed*, 183.

161. Stanley T. Williams, *The Life of Washington Irving*, 2 vols. (New York, 1935), 1:319, 321.

162. Rubin-Dorsky, *Adrift in the Old World*, 221–22.

163. Irving, *Life of George Washington* (New York, 1855).

164. Bowden, *Washington Irving*, 119.

165. Ibid., 120; 126–27. Washington Irving, *Voyages and Discoveries of the Companions of Columbus* (London, 1831).

166. William H. Prescott, *The History of the Reign of Ferdinand and Isabella the Catholic*, 3d ed. (New York, 1838).

167. He visited Paris in 1805, 1820–1821, 1823–1825, 1842, 1842, and 1844.

168. On the history of the Institute and the Academy of Sciences, see Jules Simon, *Une Académie sous le Directoire* (Paris, 1885) Ernest Seillière, *Une Académie à l'époque romantique* (Paris, 1926); Roger Hahn, *The Anatomy of a Scientific Institution: The Paris Academy of Sciences 1666–1803* (Berkeley, Calif., 1971).

169. Edmé Mentelle, *Précis d'histoire universelle* (Paris, 1798).

170. Mentelle, *Cosmographie élémentaire, divisée en parties astronomique et géographique* (Paris, 1781), 188, 194. Jean-Baptiste Delambre, *Histoire de l'astronomie du moyen âge* (Paris, 1819), v–li.

171. Antoine-Jean Letronne, *Matériaux pour servir à l'histoire du christianisme* (Paris, 1833); *Examen critique de la découverte du coeur de Saint Louis faite à la Sainte Chapelle le 15 mai 1843* (Paris, 1844).

172. Letronne, "Des opinions cosmographiques des pères de l'église," *Revue des deux mondes,* 1 (March 15, 1834): 601–33.

173. Vicomte de Santarem, *Essai sur l'histoire de la cosmographie et de la cartographie pendant le moyen âge,* 3 vols. (Paris, 1849–1852), 1:vii, cites Irving favorably.

174. Voltaire, *Dictionnaire philosophique* s.v. "Le ciel des anciens" and "Genèse"; Voltaire, *Essai sur les moeurs,* 2 vols. (Paris, 1963), chapters 9, 82, 145, 149; Voltaire, "Le chapitre des arts," *Mercure de France* (1745), 2: 837–41.

175. Etienne Bonnot de Condillac, *Cours d'étude pour l'instruction du Prince de Parme* (Parma, 1776), 5:1 speaks vaguely of the "prejudices that several philosophers" had against the round earth without specifying who or when. The Marquis de Condorcet, *Esquisse d'un tableau historique des progrès de l'esprit humain* (Paris, 1795; I use 1970 ed.), 84; 90–91. William Robertson, *View of the Progress of Society in Europe, from the Subversion of the Roman Empire, to the Beginning of the Sixteenth Century* (1769), 120–22; Denis Diderot, *Encyclopédie* s.v. "scholastique"; Benjamin Franklin, *Autobiography* (London, 1754); David Hume, *History of England* (London, 1754–1762); Henry St. John Bolingbroke (1678–1751), *Letters on the Study and Use of History* in *Works* (London, 1752).

176. Edward Gibbon, *The Decline and Fall of the Roman Empire,* 6 vols. (Boston, 1854), chapter 40, 4:73; Thomas Paine (1737–1809), *The Age of Reason* (London, 1794), 493–94.

177. Thomas Hobbes (1588–1679), *Leviathan* (London, 1651), chapter 46–47.

178. John Wilkins, *The Mathematical and Philosophical Works of the Right Reverend John Wilkins* (London, 1708; 2d ed., 1802; repr. 1970), 4–7, 109, 139, 211.

179. John Dillenberger, *Protestant Thought and Natural Science* (New York, 1960), 21–22, 30–32.

180. Galileo, "Letter to Cristina di Lorena, Granduchessa di Toscana," dated 1615, in *Galileo Galilei opere,* ed. Ferdinando Flora (Milan and Naples, 1953), 1016–28, where Galileo quotes Augustine's *In*

Genesi ad litteram, 1.21, 2.9. See Giorgio di Santillana, *The Crime of Galileo* (Chicago, 1955) and Galileo Galilei, *Dialogue on the Great World Systems* (Chicago, 1953), 12, 73.

181. Thomas Campanella, *The Defense of Galileo,* ed. and trans. Grant McColley (Northampton, Mass., 1915), 15, 35, 37, 42–44, 51.

182. Johannes Kepler, *Apologia pro Tychone contra Ursum:* in *The Birth of History and Philosophy of Science: Kepler's 'A Defence of Tycho aqainst Ursus' with Essays on its Provenance and Significance,* ed. N. Jardine (Cambridge, 1984).

183. In "L'Apologie de Raymond Sebonde," ed. Paul Porteau (Paris, 1937), 220. Montaigne says merely and correctly that "c'estoit heresie d'avouer des antipodeans (it was heresy to believe in antipodeans)." Francis Bacon, *Filum Labyrinthi,* 7 (421), *The Works of Francis Bacon,* collected and edited by James Spedding, Robert Leslie Ellis, and Douglas Denon Heath, 6 vols. (1860–1864). Giordano Bruno, *Dialoghi metafisici* in *Dialoghi italiani,* 3d ed., Florence, 1958.

184. Copernicus, *De revolutionibus orbium caelestium, On the Revolutions,* ed. Jerzy Dobrzycki, trans. Edward Rosen, 3 vols. (Krakow, 1978). The first edition of *De revolutionibus* was 1543. See Thomas S. Kuhn, *The Copernican Revolution* (Cambridge, Mass., 1957).

185. Copernicus, *De revolutionibus,* 2:5. Copernicus's own preface must not be confused with the foreword written by the Protestant divine Andreas Osiander (1498–1552). Osiander, apparently trying to smooth the way for Copernicus's reception, firmly took the position that Copernicus was writing to save the appearances rather than claiming to find the Truth through science. Osiander may have distorted Copernicus's own position in this, and Galileo's followers found his words offensive: "For these hypotheses need not be true or even probable." As John Dillenberger glosses, "It is enough if they provide a calculus which fits the observations." Many modern philosophers of science would tend to agree with Osiander. See John Dillenberger, *Protestant Thought and Natural Science: A Historical Interpretation* (New York, 1960), 42. From the other side, the papacy found the whole discussion of Lactantius offensive, and the Sacred Congregation of the Index ordered it stricken from the book; however, the first three editions of the book were issued before the order (issued March 5, 1616) could take effect.

186. The best treatment of the ideas of "Renaissance" and "Middle Ages" remains Wallace K. Ferguson, *The Renaissance in Historical Thought: Five Centuries of Interpretation* (Cambridge, Mass., 1948); See

also Giorgio Falco, *La polemica sul medio evo* (Turin, 1933; 2d ed. Naples, 1974); Marcel Beck, *Finsteres oder Romantisches Mittelalter* (Zurich, 1950); Lucie Varga, *Das Schlagwort vom "finsteren Mittelalters"* (Baden, 1932); Fred C. Robinson, "Medieval, the Middle Ages," *Speculum* 59 (1984): 745–56.

187. Ficino, quoted by Robert Nisbet, *History of the Idea of Progress* (New York, 1980), 102.

188. Theodor Mommsen, "Petrarch's Conception of the 'Dark Ages,' " *Speculum* 17 (1942): 226–42. Ferguson, *Renaissance in Historical Thought,* 8.

189. An exception was Flavio Biondo, who wrote a history of the decline of Rome from the fifth century to his own day (c. 1450); the exception proves the point: Biondo could see the period only as one of decline. Biondo's work was a direct precedent for Gibbon's *Decline and Fall of the Roman Empire* (London, 1788). Ferguson, *Renaissance in Historical Thought,* 11–12.

190. Walter Berschin, *Greek Letters and the Latin Middle Ages* (Washington, D.C., 1988), 3.

191. Ferguson, *Renaissance in Historical Thought,* 74–76. Terms used included *media tempestas, medium aevum, media aetas.* Christoph Keller (Cellarius) was a Protestant professor of history at Halle. *Historia medii aevi a temporibus Constantini Magni ad Constantinopolim a Turchia captam deducta* (Zeitz, 1688).

192. The system of dating B.C. and A.D. was invented by Denis Petain, a French Jesuit, in 1627, and the system caught on as early as 1650.

193. Bolingbroke, *Letters on the Study and the Use of History,* 1: 201.

194. Arthur Danto, *Analytical Philosophy of History* (Cambridge, 1965).

195. Howard Pyle, *Otto of the Silver Hand* (New York, 1918), 1–2.

196. Amos Funkenstein, *Theology and the Scientific Imagination: From the Middle Ages to the Seventeenth Century* (Princeton, 1986), 3, 18, 360.

197. For the contemporary shift of scientific thought away from scientific realism see Roger Jones, *Physics as Metaphor* (Minneapolis, 1982); Bruce Gregory, *Inventing Reality: Physics as Language* (New York, 1988); Owen Barfield, *Saving the Appearances: A Study in Idolatry* (London, 1957); Stephen Toulmin, *Human Understanding* (Princeton, 1972).

198. The distinction of natural science from science or knowledge in general occurred gradually: Domingo Gundisalvo, "Classification of the Sciences," in *A Source Book in Medieval Science*, ed. Edward Grant (Cambridge, Mass., 1974), 59–76; on the English scientist-bishop Robert Kilwardby in the mid-thirteenth century: James A. Weisheipl, "The Nature, Scope, and Classification of the Sciences," in *Science in the Middle Ages*, ed. David C. Lindberg (Chicago, 1978), 461–82.

199. Pierre Duhem, *Le système du monde*, 10 vols., (Paris, 1913–1959). See Funkenstein, *Theology and the Scientific Imagination*, 361–62.

200. Charles Homer Haskins, *The Renaissance of the Twelfth Century* (Cambridge, Mass., 1927).

201. Lynn Thorndike, *History of Magic and Experimental Science*, 8 vols. (New York, 1923–1958), 1:480.

202. Alexandre Koyré, *The Astronomical Revolution: Copernicus — Kepler — Borelli* (Ithaca, N.Y., 1973).

203. F. S. Betten, "Knowledge of the Sphericity of the Earth during the Earlier Middle Ages," *Catholic Historical Review* 3 (1923): 74–90.

204. Charles W. Jones, "The Flat Earth," *Thought* 9 (1934): 296–307.

205. Michael B. Foster, "The Christian Doctrine of Creation and the Rise of Modern Natural Science," *Mind* 43 (1934): 446–48.

206. George Sarton, *Introduction to the History of Science*, 3 vols. (Baltimore, 1927), 2:44–46.

207. Eva G. R. Taylor, *Ideas on the Shape, Size, and Movements of the Earth* (London, 1943).

208. Thomas S. Kuhn, *The Copernican Revolution* (Cambridge, Mass., 1957), 123. A variety of views can be found in modern historians. William H. Stahl (1908–1969), *Roman Science: Origins, Development, and Influence to the Later Middle Ages* (Madison, 1962), argues that Greek science was good, that it decayed with the Romans, and that it did not revive until the twelfth century. But Stahl, too, understood that Lactantius was an anomaly. Alistair Crombie (b. 1915), a historian of science at Oxford, perceived a decline in Roman and early medieval science with a revival in the twelfth and thirteenth centuries: Crombie, *Augustine to Galileo*, 2d ed. (Oxford, 1962).

209. See Owen Barfield, *Saving the Appearances: A Study in Idolatry* (London, 1957).

210. Woodward, "Reality, Symbolism, Time, and Space," 510–17.

211. Phillip E. Johnson, "Unbelievers Unwelcome in the Science Lab," *Los Angeles Times* (November 3, 1990): B7.

212. Christopher Lasch, "Progress: The Last Superstition," *Tikkun* 4 (1989): 27–30; Stephen Jay Gould, "The Chain of Reason vs. the Chain of Thumbs," *Natural History* (July, 1989): 12–21; J. B. Bury, *The Idea of Progress* (New York, 1932); Robert Nisbet, *History of the Idea of Progress* (New York, 1980).

213. Gould, "The Chain of Reason vs. the Chain of Thumbs," 16.

Selected Bibliography

Abetti, Giorgio. *The History of Astronomy.* New York, 1952.

Adams, George Burton. *Civilization During the Middle Ages.* New York, 1874.

Adams, Herbert B. *Columbus and His Discovery of America.* Baltimore, 1892.

Agar, William M. *Catholicism and the Progress of Science.* New York, 1940.

Altschuler, Glenn C. *Andrew Dickson White: Educator, Historian. Diplomat.* Ithaca, N.Y., 1979.

Bainton, Roland H. *George Lincoln Burr: His Life; Selections from His Writings.* Edited by Lois O. Gibbons. Ithaca, N.Y., 1943.

Beazley, Charles Raymond. *The Dawn of Modern Geography.* 3 vols. London, 1897–1906.

Beck, Marcel. *Finsteres oder romantisches Mittelalter.* 2 vols. Zurich, 1950.

Berschin, Walter. *Greek Letters and the Latin Middle Ages: From Jerome to Nicholas of Cusa.* Washington, D.C., 1988.

Betten, Francis S. "Knowledge of the Sphericity of the Earth During the Earlier Middle Ages." *Catholic Historical Review* 3 (1923): 74–90.

Blacker, Carmen, and Michael Loewe, eds. *Ancient Cosmologies.* London, 1975.

Boorstin, Daniel. *The Discoverers.* New York, 1983.

Bordin, Ruth. *Andrew Dickson White: Teacher of History.* Ann Arbor, 1958.

Bowden, Mary Weatherspoon. *Washington Irving.* Boston, 1981.

Brincken, Anna-Dorothee von den. "Die Kugelgestalt der Erde in der Kartographie des Mittelalters." *Archiv für Kulturgeschichte* 58 (1976): 77–95.

Bunbury, Edward Herbert. *A History of Ancient Geography . . . to the Fall of the Roman Empire,* 2d ed. London, 1883.

Bury, J. B. *The Idea of Progress: An Inquiry into its Origin and Growth.* New York, 1932.

Chiari, Joseph. *Christopher Columbus.* New York, 1979.

Collis, John Stewart. *Christopher Columbus.* London, 1976.

Corsi, Pietro. *Science and Religion: Baden Powell and the Anglican Debate 1800–1860.* Cambridge, 1988.

Crombie, Alistair C. *Augustine to Galileo: The History of Science,* 2d ed. Oxford, 1962.

———. *Robert Grosseteste and the Origins of Experimental Science, 1100–1700,* 2d ed. Oxford, 1962.

Dampier, William Cecil. *A History of Science and Its Relations with Philosophy and Religion.* Cambridge, 1929.

Delambre, Jean-Baptiste. *Histoire de l'astronomie au moyen âge.* Paris, 1819.

Dicks, D. R. *Early Greek Astronomy to Aristotle.* Ithaca, N.Y., 1970.

Dillenberger, John. *Protestant Thought and Natural Science: A Historical Interpretation.* New York, 1960.

Dobrzycki, Jerzy, ed. *The Reception of Copernicus' Heliocentric Theory.* Boston, 1972.

Draper, John W. *History of the Conflict between Religion and Science.* New York, 1874.

———. *History of the Intellectual Development of Europe.* New York and London, 1863.

Dreyer, J.L.E. *A History of Astronomy from Thales to Kepler,* 2d ed. New York, 1953.

Duhem, Pierre. *Le système du monde: Histoire des doctrines cosmologiques de Platon à Copernic.* 10 vols. Paris, 1913–1959.

Falco, Giorgio. *La polemica sul medio evo,* 2d ed. Naples, 1974.

Farrington, Benjamin. *Greek Science: Its Meaning for Us.* Harmondsworth, 1944.

Fernandez-Armesto, Felipe. *Before Columbus: Exploration and Colonization from the Mediterranean to the Atlantic, 1229–1492.* Philadelphia, 1987.

————. *Columbus and the Conquest of the Impossible.* New York, 1974.

Ferguson, Wallace K. *The Renaissance in Historical Thought: Five Centuries of Interpretation.* New York, 1948.

Fiske, John. *The Discovery of America.* 2 vols. Boston, 1892.

Fleming, Donald. *John William Draper and the Religion of Science.* Philadelphia, 1950.

Funkenstein, Amos. *Theology and the Scientific Imagination: From the Middle Ages to the Seventeenth Century.* Princeton, 1986.

Gatto, Ludovico. *Viaggio intorno al concetto di medioevo: Profilo di storia della storiografia medievale.* Rome, 1977.

————. *Medioevo voltairiano.* Rome, 1972.

Gould, Stephen Jay. "The Chain of Reason vs. the Chain of Thumbs." *Natural History* (July, 1979): 12–21.

Grant, Edward. *A Source Book in Medieval Science.* Cambridge, Mass., 1974.

————. *Physical Science in the Middle Ages.* New York, 1971.

Granzotto, Gianni. *Christopher Columbus.* New York, 1985.

Haber, Francis C. *The Age of the World: Moses to Darwin.* Baltimore, 1959.

Hall, Norman F. and Lucia K. B. Hall, "Is the War between Science and Religion Over?" *The Humanist* 46 (May/June 1986): 26–28.

Harley, J. B. and David Woodward. *The History of Cartography: Cartography in Prehistoric, Ancient, and Medieval Europe and the Mediterranean.* Chicago, 1987.

Haskins, Charles Homer. *Studies in the History of Mediaeval Science.* Cambridge, Mass., 1924.

Hedges, William L. *Washington Irving: An American Study, 1802–1832.* Baltimore, 1965.

Heers, Jacques. *Christophe Colomb.* Paris, 1981.

Hooykaas, Reijer. *Religion and the Rise of Modern Science.* Grand Rapids, Mich., 1972.

Irving, Washington. *A History of New York.* Edited by Michael L. Black and Nancy B. Black. Boston, 1984.

————. *The Life and Voyages of Christopher Columbus.* Edited by John Harmon McElroy. Boston, 1981.

Jane, Cecil. *Select Documents Illustrating the Four Voyages of Columbus.* 2 vols. London, 1930–1933.

Jardine, Nicholas. *The Birth of History and Philosophy of Science: Kepler's A Defence of Tycho against Ursus, with Essays on its Provenance and Significance.* Cambridge, 1984.

Jones, Charles W. "The Flat Earth." *Thought* 9 (1934): 296–307.

Kimble, George H. T. *Geography in the Middle Ages.* London, 1938.

Kingsley, Charles. *Scientific Lectures and Essays.* London, 1880.

Koyré, Alexandre. *The Astronomical Revolution: Copernicus — Kepler — Borelli.* Ithaca, N.Y., 1973.

Kuhn, Thomas S. *The Copernican Revolution: Planetary Astronomy in the Development of Western Thought.* Cambridge, Mass., 1957.

Langlois, Charles-V. *La Connaissance de la nature du monde au moyen âge d'après les écrits français à l'usage des laics.* Paris, 1927.

Lelewel, Joachim. *Géographie du moyen âge.* 4 vols. Brussels, 1850–1852.

Letronne, Antoine-Jean. "Des opinions cosmographiques des pères de l'église." *Revue des deux mondes* (March 15, 1834): 601–33.

Lindberg, David C. ed. *Science in the Middle Ages.* Chicago, 1978.

Lindberg, David C. and Ronald L. Numbers, eds. *God and Nature: Historical Essays on the Encounter Between Science and Christianity.* Berkeley, Calif., 1986.

———. "Beyond War and Peace: A Reappraisal of the Encounter between Christianity and Science." *Church History* 55 (1986): 338–54.

Madariaga, Salvador de. *Vida del muy magnifico señor Don Cristobal Colon,* 7th ed. Buenos Aires, 1959.

Mentelle, Edmé. *Cosmographie élémentaire, divisée en parties astronomique et géographique.* Paris, 1781.

Mommsen, Theodor E. "Petrarch's Conception of the 'Dark Ages.' " *Speculum* 17 (1942): 226–42.

Moore, James R. *The Post-Darwinian Controversies: A Study of the Protestant Struggle to Come to Terms with Darwin in Great Britain and America, 1870–1900.* Cambridge, 1979.

Morison, Samuel Eliot. *Admiral of the Ocean Sea.* Boston, 1942.

———. *The European Discovery of America.* New York, 1974.

———. *The European Discovery of America: The Northern Voyages.* New York, 1971.

Navarrete, Martin Fernandez de. *Coleccion de los viajes y descubrimientos que hicierion por mar los Españoles desde fines del siglo xv.* 5 vols. Madrid, 1825–1837.

Neugebauer, Otto. *The Exact Sciences in Antiquity,* 2d ed. Providence, 1957.

Newton, Robert R. *Medieval Chronicles and the Rotation of the Earth.* Baltimore, 1972.

Nisbet, Robert. *History of the Idea of Progress.* New York, 1980.

O'Neil, W. M. *Early Astronomy from Babylonia to Copernicus.* Sydney, 1986.

Orr, M. A. *Dante and the Early Astronomers.* London, 1914.

O'Gorman, Edmundo. *The Invention of America: An Inquiry into the Historical Nature of the New World and the Meaning of its History.* Bloomington, 1961.

Pannekoek, A. *A History of Astronomy.* New York, 1961.

Parry, J. H. *The Discovery of the Sea.* London, 1974.

Penrose, Boies. *Travel and Discovery in the Renaissance, 1420–1620.* Cambridge, Mass., 1952.

Pernoud, Régine. *Pour en finir avec le moyen âge.* Paris, 1977.

Randles, W.G.L. *De la terre plate au globe terrestre: Une mutation épistémologique rapide (1480–1520).* Paris, 1980. Translated as *The Classical Tradition and the Americas* (Tübingen and Boston, 1992).

Raven, Charles E. *Natural Religion and Christian Theology.* 2 vols. Cambridge, 1953.

Robinson, Fred C. "Medieval, the Middle Ages." *Speculum* 59 (1984): 745–56.

Rubin-Dorsky, Jeffrey. *Adrift in the Old World: The Psychological Pilgrimage of Washinqton Irving.* Chicago, 1988.

Russell, Jeffrey B. "Saint Boniface and the Eccentrics." *Church History* 33 (1964): 235–47.

Santarem, Vicomte de. *Essai sur l'histoire de la cosmographie et de la cartographie pendant le moyen âge.* 3 vols. Paris, 1849–1852.

———. *Recherches historiques, critiques, et bibliographiques sur Améric Vespuce et ses voyages.* Paris, n.d.

Sarton, George. *Introduction to the History of Science,* 3 vols. Baltimore, 1927.

Seillière, Ernest. *Une Académie à l'époque romantique.* Paris, 1926.

Shipley, Maynard. *The War on Modern Science: A Short History of the Fundamentalist Attacks on Evolution and Modernism.* New York, 1927.

Simon, Jules. *Une Académie sous le Directoire.* Paris, 1885.

Simpson, James Young. *Landmarks in the Struggle Between Science and Religion.* London, 1925.

Singer, Charles, ed. *Studies in the History and Method of Science,* 2d ed. London, 1955.

Tattersall, Jill. "Sphere or Disc? Allusions to the Shape of the Earth in Some Twelfth-Century and Thirteenth-Century French Works." *Modern Language Review* 76 (1981): 31–46.

Taylor, Eva G. R. *Ideas on the Shape, Size. and Movements of the Earth.* London, 1943.

Thomson, James Oliver. *History of Ancient Geography.* Cambridge, 1948.

Thorndike, Lynn. *The Sphere of Sacrobosco and Its Commentators.* Chicago, 1949.

Tobler, Waldo. "Medieval Distortions: The Projections of Ancient Maps." *Annals of the Association of American Geographers* 56 (1966): 351–60.

Todhunter, I. *William Whewell D.D., Master of Trinity College, Cambridge: An Account of His Writings with Selections from His Literary and Scientific Correspondence.* London, 1876.

Toulmin, Stephen and June Goodfield. *The Fabric of the Heavens.* New York, 1961.

Tozer, H. F. *A History of Ancient Geography.* Cambridge, 1897.

Van Helden, Albert. *Measuring the Universe: Cosmic Dimensions from Aristarchus to Halley.* Chicago, 1985.

Varga, Lucie. *Das Schlagwort vom "finsteren" Mittelalter.* Baden, 1932.

Wagenknecht, Edward. *Washington Irving: Moderation Displayed.* New York, 1962.

Westman, Robert S. "The Duhemian Historiographical Project." *Synthèse* 38 (1990): 261–72.

———. "La préface de Copernic au pape: Esthétique humaniste et réforme de l'église." *History and Technology* 4 (1987): 365–84.

Whewell, William. *History of the Inductive Sciences from the Earliest to the Present Time.* 2 vols. New York, 1897.

White, Andrew Dickson. *The Autobiography of Andrew Dickson White.* New York, 1905.

———. *A History of the Warfare of Science with Theology in Christendom.* 2 vols. New York, 1896.

Williams, Stanley T. *The Life of Washington Irving.* 2 vols. New York, 1935.

Windle, Bertram C. A. *The Church and Science.* London, 1917.

Winstedt, Eric Otto, ed. *The Christian Topography of Cosmas Indico-pleustes.* Cambridge, 1909.

Wolska-Conus, Wanda. *La topographie chrétienne de Cosmas Indicopleustès: Théologie et science au VIe siècle.* Paris, 1962.

Woodward, David. "Reality, Symbolism, Time, and Space in Medieval World Maps." *Annals of the Association of American Geographers* 75 (1985): 510–21.

Wright, John Kirtland. *The Geographical Lore of the Time of the Crusades: A Study in the History of Medieval Science and Tradition in Western Europe.* New York, 1925.

Index

About the Author

JEFFREY BURTON RUSSELL is Professor of History at the University of California, Santa Barbara. He is a frequent contributor to history volumes, including the *Handbook of World History* and *The Transformation of the Western World*. Dr. Russell has also written fifteen previous books and contributed articles to scholarly journals, such as *History Today* and *Christianity Today*.